REASON & TOLERANCE

An Argument Asserting the Necessity for an

AMERICAN
CIVIC REVOLUTION

Including

TEN AMENDMENTS

to Save

AMERICA

W. DAVIS JONES, IV

RALEIGH, NORTH CAROLINA

MMX

Fear not dear child of darkness
For though you cannot see
Events to pass before you
Are surely meant to be

Although you stumble blindly
Your life in disarray
The strength exists within you
The trouble to belay

Have faith in God Almighty
Your power he doth know
The dormant strength within you
His power to bestow

Although loving, kind, benevolent
He placed us on this earth
To work out for ourselves a life
Balanced of sorrow, toil and mirth

Reason & Tolerance: An Argument Asserting the Necessity for an American Civic Revolution

White Oak Publishing Company
P. O. Box 12952
Raleigh, North Carolina 27605-2952

This book is dedicated to young Americans who are coming of age and should never forget:

Freedom requires responsibility
and must ever be defended.

Contents

Foreword

We all have opinions that are based on something: they are usually emotional reactions to what we see on TV, read in papers, hear on the radio, or discuss with friends and coworkers. This is why marketing has become a science and a highly paid component of every business and political campaign. Emotional reactions can be manipulated, and therefore money drives politics.

In the 1990s, I was outraged by U.S. politics. I didn't understand why the nation as a whole was not outraged. With changes taking place in my country, that at the very least reflected abandonment of values and at the worst was placing the United States and our way of life in jeopardy, I felt a need to understand why I believed what I believed in terms of history and the principles upon which our nation rests. Thus began a project that has culminated in this book.

What I learned was that principles, developed through reasoned discourse and preserved by institutions throughout history, provide the foundation upon which societies create stable and secure environments in which people may live meaningful lives. When those principles are abandoned, only evil or failure can result.

This is why we see a pattern throughout history of the rise and fall of nations and cultures. Human behavior is influenced by our environment, and when the environment of an evolving culture reaches certain levels of affluence, our instincts for survival are compromised. The importance of principles that created and maintain that affluence are marginalized or forgotten altogether.

I spent more than two years studying and writing a book entitled *Collective Wisdom: The American Peoples' Right of Power*. This was a lengthy book that included details about history and U.S. case studies. It was interesting to me but not to anyone else. However, the process helped me to understand what I believed and why I believed it from a historical and reasoned point of view. It clarified most of my beliefs and changed my mind about certain issues. Most of all, it helped me to understand the U.S. Constitution and how the courts have made a mess of its interpretation, placing our nation at peril.

The Constitution consists of principles that serve as the foundation on which our nation was established. Those principles, by definition, have not changed, and the

Constitution, which is itself a legal document, is the precedent that trumps all precedents and the single and the Constitution is the precedent that trumps all precedents and the single legal document that the United States cannot exist without.

Marginalizing the principles upon which a nation rests has been a destructive behavior throughout history. When principles are abandoned, civilizations and the nations they have created go downhill quickly.

I have no interest in the United States ceasing to exist or becoming subordinate to foreign powers. Therefore, the Constitution and the principles it espouses must be recognized and upheld. This core belief is based on thousands of years of human reason and is the ultimate conclusion to my quest.

It was not enough to feel a sense of personal accomplishment and have confidence in my positions and votes, but I needed to share what I discovered and communicate those ideas and the supporting arguments. *Collective Wisdom* was not the vehicle to accomplish this, so I set out to write a concise pamphlet. That pamphlet has turned into this book, and although *Reason & Tolerance* has a good deal of information, it can be read in one to two sittings. I have tried hard to be true to reason and not be swayed by specific issues, partisanship, or politics. It is almost impossible, but I have done my best.

My hope is that *Reason & Tolerance* may pique the reader's interest in reacting less and thinking more. If enough Americans understand the need to take these actions while considering those worthy of our votes, America is sure to continue to be the force for good throughout the world for decades, if not centuries, to come.

W. Davis Jones
Raleigh, North Carolina
July 2010

Introduction

*H*ISTORY teaches us that civilizations rise and fall in cycles. Perpetuation of government by the people and preservation of liberty for future generations may only be realized through an American Civic Revolution.

American work ethic is as strong as it has ever been. The work has become easier, and the quality of life has improved substantially since 1776, especially for working-class Americans. However, we are not as democratic or independent as we used to be. Our family support system has largely been replaced by federal entitlements and community support by federal programs. Liberty was once defined as freedom from government interference, but today, American liberty is freedom from responsibility.

Our democratic republic has been diluted by the courts, and political correctness has enabled minority and extreme interests to subvert rule by the majority.

The laws of human nature and physics dictate movement away from pressure whether from external forces of heat, wind, and water, or internal forces of guilt, anger, and frustration. It is natural to avoid unpleasant circumstances, and perfectly human to put off that which one is not forced to deal with today.

Courage is the human will to act in the face of adversity. We celebrate the courage demonstrated by our founding fathers under threat of death, treason, or ruin. We honor those who fought and died to preserve our safety and liberty. We admire Americans who choose unforgiving professions to protect our communities and save our lives in moments of crisis and tragedy. Individual freedom, republican government, and national sovereignty have been placed at great risk in spite of the sacrifices made by our American forbearers over the past two hundred years. Do Americans today have the desire and the courage necessary to defend the founding principles of our nation, or is our Constitution headed for the trash heap of history? Are we prepared to admit failure of self-government, call for a constitutional convention, and rewrite the Constitution to vastly expand federal powers to legalize the current government, or will we reaffirm the authority of our Constitution and realign our federal government with the organization, powers, and principles the Constitution establishes? We cannot continue to display disdain and disrespect for the document of our founding. We cannot forsake a future of liberty for our children. To guard against the erosive forces of politics and the atrophy of freedom from disregard, Americans must act, and we must act must act now.

Utility of Sovereignty

*A*MERICAN pre-eminence is inextricably tied to a sense of responsibility to mankind, the elimination of exploitation, and the encouragement of human dignity. American sovereignty and influence in the world is a direct extension of the founding fathers' recognition of divine rights and a Constitution that allows the exercise thereof. Loss of the belief in a divine being, national sovereignty, constitutional integrity, or individual freedoms will undermine national interests and have a devastating impact on the world at large.

Religious freedom has driven many immigrants to American shores. Recognition of divine rights provided the reasoning for independence and a government and society based on a universal moral order.

1

Three of the world's great religions evolved from the recognition of monotheism, the God of Moses. According to Abram Leon Sachar in *A History of the Jews*, "To Moses Yahweh was indissolubly bound up with the lives of men and the moral order of the universe . . . To break the law, then, was more than a crime against society; it was a sin against Yahweh." Having been led to freedom during the Exodus, the Israelites disobeyed Moses, were banished to the desert for forty years, and were taught that there is no freedom without responsibility. The story of Moses establishes a universal moral order, confirms man's divine right to freedom, and the necessity for individual responsibility. Like the Constitution, this is all written down in the Ten Commandments so that we will not forget.

In the sixth century, the prophet Jeremiah came to perceive the personal nature of God. God existed in the heart of man and every form of nature, linking all men and all things. Each man perceived and appealed to God in his own way, but the nature of this personal God made man responsible to himself as well as to all of society.

As the Bible began to be printed in English and read on a widespread basis for the first time in the seventeenth century, the people read for themselves the word of God and began to challenge the divine right of Kings and the Church. Pilgrims saw landing in America as their Exodus from spiritual enslavement and delivery to their promised land. Discovery of the New World presented an opportunity for man to live and worship freely through a personal God, free from persecution from kings and feudal authority.

During the Revolution, Americans wanted to free themselves from the tyranny of the Crown to create a new nation under God. When Thomas Jefferson wrote, ". . . all men are created equal, that they are endowed by their Creator with certain unalienable Rights, that among these are Life, Liberty and the pursuit of Happiness," he was reaching to the God of Moses for the moral authority for the actions the colonists were preparing to take and establishing a moral basis from which law would govern society. God is irrevocably woven into the fabric of our nation and its institutions and must always be so as long as the nation exists.

Mankind's social and dependent nature binds all men. Civilization permits the realization of human potential. Civilizations have an optimal size and effective lifespan that may best be realized through slow and steady growth. Stagnation or upheaval from rapid growth or internal changes results in instability.

A nation is defined by a common bond among the citizenry and borders within which laws are established and enforced by the citizens. The health and future for a nation is subject to the preservation of national integrity. An uncontrolled influx of illegal immigrants (U.S. Constitution, art. 1, sec. 8, and art. 4, sec. 4,) changes the characteristics of a nation. National interests are diluted or fractionalized, undermining common interests among the citizenry. A steady flow of legal immigration reinvigorates a nation with new ideas, energy, and appreciation for the special characteristics that spurred the desire to immigrate. Moderation in immigration policy insures a timely assimilation of those new citizens and their families. For twenty years, the United States has allowed levels of legal immigration that exceeded one million per year by 2005. During this same time period, the federal government failed to curb the flow of illegal immigrants by enforcing existing federal law. This flood of immigration is felt through conflict among citizens, language barriers, and costs imposed on local governments. A nation without borders cannot enforce laws, protect resources, or provide security, leading to instability and internal conflict. To promote individual freedom, the federal government must, first and foremost, secure our borders while continually working to minimize friction among nations.

While some nations share our recognition of divine right and democratic values, many do not. The United Nations was formed to provide a forum for the world's nations to address mutual interests and concerns. However, the disparate interests of member nations remains substantially greater than any common bond, so a world government cannot succeed in these times, and any effort or policy to subordinate U.S. policy or the Constitution to international law is contrary to our history and undermines our nation's interests. U.S. national sovereignty is necessary for the perpetuation of Western civilization and the continued pursuit of human potential.

Different types of government have different purposes. True democracy is defined as a group in which all decisions are made equally among every member of the group. The Greek concept of *ho buolomenos* is one in which all members of a group are considered capable and chosen by lottery for specific responsibilities. This system of randomly selecting individuals from a pool of citizens of equal ability is practiced today in the U.S. jury system. Once the number and geographic area of a society become too great, true democracy can no longer be sustained, and therefore a republic is formed. Citizens then elect individuals based on merit to reasonably exercise power on their behalf. Representation based on individual merit requires responsible citizens to support representatives of character to guard against ambitious men.

Once a government's provisions for a secure and stable environment have been balanced adequately against individual freedoms, the more ubiquitous that government becomes, the less freedom the people enjoy. A constitutional government is one in which the people extend limited power to the government to meet collective needs without encroaching upon the ability of the people to exercise their freedoms. A government consisting of ambitious men ignores this balance by exceeding constitutional authority, threatening the legitimacy of the government and the nation. Constitutional integrity is essential to the survival of the United States.

Man was placed on earth by a benevolent God and blessed with the gift of thought. Descartes' statement "I think therefore I am" gives rise to the understanding and exercise of individual free will. Individuals have the free will to do what they want, when and where they want. However, John Locke, the founder of liberalism and the philosopher most closely studied by the founding fathers, believed that liberty in a society was not the freedom for every person to do anything they wish, any time or any place, but, "having a standing rule to live by, common to every one of that society, and made by legislative power." Individuals may no longer exercise absolute free will but, in a society, must subordinate some of their interests for the benefit of the group as a whole.

There are many forms of freedom in a free society. Labor is the exercise of one's freedom to provide for immediate survival or security through the accumulation of property. Economic principles dictate that when supply of labor goes up, wages go down. If a man's labor is his freedom to live and support his family, suppression of wages is suppression of freedom. Individual freedom is best served for the vast majority of Americans when the supply of workers trails that of demand maximizing individual opportunity and wages without crippling economic growth. An uncontrolled influx of immigration floods the labor force, suppressing wages and freedom.

Government has the duty through law to protect life and property. In early America, citizens with property were considered free from dependence on others and therefore were a minority that held special civic privileges. Denying a person property is denial of freedom, so specific precautions were put in place by the Constitution to guard against the majority taking property from the minority. Congress was created with a Senate and a House of Representatives (U.S. Constitution, art. 1). The House members were elected directly by the people of each state to represent the interests of the majority. The Senate was modeled on the British Parliament House of Lords that represented, and guarded, the propertied class. The dynamic of the Senate was substantially changed in 1913 with the passage of the Seventeenth Amendment which changed elections for Senators from state legislatures to a popular vote.

Financial debt is the exercise of free will to leverage one's future labor for immediate benefit. Freedom from debt is a personal choice that most Americans have abandoned, diminishing the future value of our labor and therefore our sovereignty.

We have established that freedom cannot exist without responsibility. Individuals who have transferred their responsibility to the government have done so at the unthinkable price of subordinating free will to government dictates. One may believe he is trading one type of freedom for more desirable ones such as freedom from decisions or the need to provide labor to sustain life. Others may believe that the greater the government responsibility, the freer the individual is to do what he wishes, when he wishes and where he wishes, despite the increase in government dictates. This contradicts the assertion that this condition cannot exist in a free society, because freedom without responsibility is chaos, leading to destruction of the very society the government was created to sustain.

Individuals practice free will and therefore, in a free society, equality in thought and labor is unattainable because every individual is unique. A society may strive to promote equality through liberty, opportunity, and personal dignity, but government cannot mandate equality in ability or property. One result of free will is the individual application of labor, whether to study or work. Labor provides the means by which ownership, and therefore security, is achieved. Individuals may exercise their free will to provide labor to create property that provides security, which represents individual freedom.

A government is responsible for providing a secure environment in which society may thrive. However an individual's right to exercise free will makes him directly responsible for his property and security. Government receives revenue through taxes on individual labor and property. The government cannot impose taxes to provide property or individual security to some without denying freedom to others. The burden rests with the individual to act in his own best interest with the resources available. As a nation, we must determine what role, if any, the federal government should take in providing resources to individuals to improve their circumstances, especially in light of the fact that the Constitution does not enumerate this federal power, or if this responsibility should be retained by members of a moral society through state and local governments, churches, and volunteerism.

Although money never solved any problem, our nation has increasingly and arbitrarily identified freedom as money, thereby reducing a sweeping philosophical concept to a base and vulgar application. Does money really represent freedom and solutions, or does choice and the exercise of free will? National debt is the expenditure of the labor of future generations and, therefore, our children's freedom. Taxes are essentially the collection of labor, so we seek freedom from unreasonable taxes. As entitlements grow, individuals who become dependent on those entitlements subordinate their freedom to government dictates. Government entitlements strip an individual of self-sufficiency and responsibility and therefore self-worth and dignity. Debt, taxes, and entitlements deny individual and collective freedoms and threaten our families, democracy, and national sovereignty.

The concept of "liberty" evolved over centuries with varying definitions based on moral, social, or political applications. Early understandings of liberty meant the ability to engage in certain economic activities. Moral application concerned "freedom from sin," while in a civic or secular sense, reasonable laws created freedom through education and an orderly society. By the time of the American Revolution, liberty was protection from tyranny or the abusive exercise of power. In the United States today, the concept of freedom has shifted. No longer is "freedom" considered protection from the abusive exercise of power but from individual responsibility and personal risk. The courts have placed specific and narrow special interests before the interest of the collective whole. The people have decided they are "entitled" not only from their government but from society at large. Insurance products are considered a panacea for risks, but they have usurped Americans' practice of "saving for a rainy day" and in doing, so citizens relinquish ownership and control of those assets. Among some people, freedom is the elimination of all social restrictions. This shift in the perception and application of freedom conflicts with the principles upon which this nation was founded and threatens our society and our relationship to our founding documents and future.

The Constitution was designed to create and protect both national and individual sovereignty. The diminution of either is contrary to the principles upon which the United States was founded, threatens the American standard for human dignity, and undermines our lawful rights, ability to enjoy liberty, and exercise our right to the pursuit of happiness.

Nature of Man and Government

G OVERNMENT that best reflects the divine nature of man provides an environment in which mankind's potential may best be pursued through freedom and opportunity.

The challenge of civilized man is to harness his natural instincts through strength of character to participate in a peaceful, structured, and productive society. Mans' basic instinct is survival: the need for food and shelter. As men form communities for mutual support of these needs, time for idleness, and therefore thought, evolve, including activities beyond the immediate needs of survival. Thought leads to a desire to understand the world and the meaning of existence.

Man is subject to temptation, which leads to

selfishness. An individual may instinctively demonstrate visceral behavior for survival, but in a community with relative security, it is necessary for this instinctive behavior to be superseded by virtues that contribute to the health of the community. This transition must first be made in thought, the understanding of trust and practice of skepticism, and then action.

Although trust is desirable and necessary, skepticism preserves a heightened and healthy sense of awareness and the instinctual "fight or flight" response. In a civilized society, this skepticism must be used to filter information, observe first hand, and think for oneself.

Man believes in a higher being, and if he doesn't, he believes in self. Belief in God reflects a person's humility and a belief that man is not alone and may reach out for assistance. This is consistent with a community whose members support one another. One who believes only in self is alone. Narcissism strips an individual of resources and heightens skepticism. It contributes to arrogance and undermines ones' ability to consider others before oneself.

Men placed in positions of power suffer heightened temptations that require the greatest strength of character. Therefore, those we elect to office should be the most trustworthy and of the strongest character. Nonetheless, when people do not preserve a healthy level of skepticism and allow themselves to be deceived, charlatans make their way into office. Even those who are elected and have the best intentions, as part of a political body over which responsibility can be distributed, can more easily subordinate their values and justify undesirable behavior. The longer one stays in office, the greater the temptations and the responsibility of constituents to free him of that temptation by bringing that individual home.

It is stated in the first essay of "Brutus" (1787), a series of letters critiquing the proposed Constitution, "Men are apt to be deceived both with respect to their own dispositions and those of others. Though this truth is proved by almost every page of the history of nations, to wit, that power lodged in the hands of rulers to be used at discretion, is almost always exercised to the oppression of the people, and the aggrandizement of themselves."

All men are subject to temptation and must be diligent in order to protect the community. "Cato," another article challenging the proposed federal government written on Nov. 27, 1787, reads, "...that the progress of a commercial society begets luxury, the parent of inequality, the foe to virtue, and the enemy to restraint."

The nature of man must be contained through the exercise of individual discipline reinforced by elections. A strong nation is protected by hard-working, humble people of strong character that recognize, value, and demand virtuous behavior of elected representatives.

"Brutus" continues, "...it is a truth confirmed by the unerring experience of ages, that every man, and every body of men, invested with power, are ever disposed to increase it, and to acquire a superiority over everything that stands in their way." American history reaffirms this "unerring experience of ages." The federal government has increasingly taken Americans' money, decisions, and responsibilities and will never return those freedoms willingly. During times of war, budgets are expanded to cover those costs, but following the conflict, budgets never return to previous levels of spending. Since 1937, the federal government has increasingly centralized money and decisions in an effort to move from a free to a collective society in which freedoms are taken from those with wealth through taxes and from those without wealth through dependence.

In 1787, James Madison wrote, "In all Government

there is a power which is capable of oppressive exercise . . . In popular Governments the danger lies in an undue sympathy among individuals composing a majority and a want of responsibility in the majority of the minority." Sympathy is not a responsibility of government but that of individuals and communities to be expressed through churches, civic organizations, neighbors supporting neighbors, and families helping families. This dynamic has been largely stripped by the federal government's ferocious appetite for more money. The engineered federal programs never work as intended and starve the more efficient and effective private efforts of resources.

A moral society must recognize and maintain relative affluence between segments of the population. When the gap between the dispossessed and the affluent becomes too great, excessive or flagrant tension mounts. This dynamic naturally encourages societies to stay in balance for the benefit of all—before revolution leads to violence and radical change or collapse of the nation. Effective change is driven by the people, not by government, as evidenced by civil rights, the rise of unions to protect the worker, and the growing understanding in corporate culture of how employee well-being benefits the bottom line.

In a free society, government should not control the private sector. However, government does create, endorse, or regulate entities such as corporations, the U.S. Federal Reserve, and interstate commerce. Although free markets promote competition, ensuring desired products at reasonable prices, government makes the rules by which everyone plays. Rules that promote balance in markets, such as antitrust laws, and society, such as free and mandatory education, are desirable if they apply to all equally. These government rules should promote an environment of equal opportunity before the fact rather than redistributing wealth after the fact through taxes and entitlements.

There are limits to the effective size of a republic, just as there are limits to the effective size of a democracy. A constitutional government is a limited government by definition, because a constitution defines the structure, organization, functions, and powers of the government. Uncontrolled government growth and ever-increasing power cannot be a constitutional government, and a self-sustaining government is not a republic.

People with shared interests are drawn to one another

to form groups, tribes, villages, cities, and societies. The shared interests upon which the United States was established are the divine rights of equality, life, liberty, and the pursuit of happiness. Man can never achieve but must simply recognize divine perfection as the standard toward which to strive. Most of the major internal conflicts throughout American history have come from society's growing pains associated with continually learning and striving toward this stated perfection. This process will never cease, and the standard for human dignity will continue to improve as long as the United States remains a free, constitutional, democratic republic.

How do Americans define the perfection toward which we wish to strive as a nation? Different ideologies, political parties, and special interests exist, but before the brawl for power and money, what are the principles that define the ideals to which we may all agree? Can the ideals an individual may strive to emulate be shared by the nation as a whole?

We return to the universal moral order of the founding fathers and Moses. The Ten Commandments represented the first written words of God and defined the behavior expected of individuals and society. Religions and cultures all over the world have developed moral standards for millennia, all of which share common aspects. These behaviors have been expressed generally in terms of desired behaviors, or virtues, and undesired behaviors, or vices. Virtues include chastity, temperance, charity, diligence, patience, kindness, and humility. On the other hand, vices can generally be defined as anything in excess. The seven deadly sins include pride or hubris, from which all other vices derive; extravagance or unrestrained excess; gluttony, which is overconsumption or wastefulness; greed or avarice, which is excess wealth; sloth, neglect, or failing to fulfill responsibilities; wrath or hatred; and envy, which is the desire for material goods or jealousy of anything lacked.

Since World War II and the United States' rise as a world power, the nation has been prideful. Pride is good to an extent, but as stated, anything extreme or in excess is harmful and destructive. Has America's rise to world power been followed by excess in consumption, wastefulness, desire for wealth, shirking responsibility or desire for more by individuals, the nation, or both? The answer is clearly yes. As a society, we have devalued God in our lives, placed self before marriage and family, and accepted violence and perversion in entertainment and public discourse. The U.S. government has assumed the full range of characteristics, known as vices, which are undesirable behaviors in man and much more so in a government. While America's demonstration of charity and compassion around the world is unequaled throughout history and is the standard for which Americans are admired, if our government treats the world virtuously and its own people with visceral contempt, is the nation healthy? Can it survive, and if so, for how long? If the government covets its citizens free will, that government has sinned against its own people, demonstrated a behavior forbidden by God and society, and must be removed.

The lack of civility leads to behavior contrary to the interests of an ordered society. Rudeness, lack of respect for elders, vandalism, drunkenness, and aggressive behavior are a few of the characteristics attributed to incivility. In America, we have failed to do for our children what our parents did for us. Today, demonstrations of respect are scorned in favor of acts of arrogance and vulgarity. Vandalism is accepted whether of property or reputation. The Internet has become a cesspool of incivility with participants unwilling to police themselves even to the most basic of standards. Is there anyone who really believes that *paparazzi* have the right to relentlessly abuse the objects of their frenzy? We have excused leaders who promote incivility and entertainment that promotes indecency. We have accepted contradiction and insincerity in character and discourse. We must act as individuals and a nation to reassert our understanding and practice of virtue and civility.

We must be no less diligent in policing the activities of our government. Locke believed that government should be limited to providing security to protect as opposed to creating "life, liberty, and estates." America's trend toward collectivism is the government trying to create what some perceive as liberty through denial of responsibility. We have determined that the government's attempt to transfer wealth to achieve economic equality is unattainable in a society in which men exercise free will.

The founding fathers challenged legal and government interference that obstructed individual advancement. Americans have continued to remove obstacles to inequality and injustice, and the whole of American society has benefitted. A transition from removing obstacles to implementing programs is a shift from individual opportunity and advancement to individual dependence.

An effective government is an energetic one best represented by new ideas and action. A republic with an ever-growing government becomes increasingly rigid and ineffective. Some may argue that a good federal program should be made available to all Americans, but all federal programs are limited, because they cannot address specific regional or local needs. Americans of southern California have very little in common with Americans from Appalachia. They differ in heritage, food, speech patterns, work ethic, career choices, job opportunities, family relationships, education, hairdos, clothing, etc. The only way any federal program can be implemented equally across the nation is by giving out money, which promotes avarice in government. Handing out money hobbles, undermines, degrades, and strips a person of self-sufficiency and does nothing to move the person forward. Money is never the solution to any problem, and the pattern of a perpetually ravenous and benevolent government is the antithesis of democracy.

America's greatest successes have not been a function

of money but of initiative, innovation, and personal courage. The tide was turned in the American Revolution when British Colonel Ferguson posted a demanding and threatening letter in the mountains of Appalachia. The Over-the-Mountain men took exception to this demand and took up their hunting rifles. They defeated Ferguson and his professional British troops at King's Mountain, followed a year later by the defeat of the British at Yorktown. America expanded across the continent, not by handing out money but by opening the West for those willing to claim it. The Civil War was not fought with money but with men's lives, often in ragged uniforms, defending fortifications dug from the earth with bare hands. World War II was won through the enormous industrial capability developed by private enterprise during the latter part of the nineteenth century.

The nation shifted course in 1937 from the American model of individual achievement to the European model of collectivism. Americans allowed one man, Associate Justice Owen Roberts (who inexplicably reversed his constitutional philosophy overnight) to change the course of the greatest nation in history and initiate the erosion of our freedoms and the march toward collectivism. By subordinating his intellectual and constitutional scholarship to political pressure, Roberts provided the fifth and deciding swing vote that ruled Franklin D. Roosevelt's New Deal to be constitutional.

In a constitutional democracy, how and why have we allowed five justices to usurp the principles of the Constitution and the power of the people? Roberts' surrender to political pressures enabled the creation of the pay-as-you-go Social Security system; this one-hundred-year-old Ponzi scheme has placed our nation on the path toward insolvency. Those on the front end received benefits without having contributed funds and Americans in 2030 and beyond will pay into the program throughout their careers but receive little or nothing in return. Pyramid schemes are illegal in the United States except when run by the government. By the same token, politicians from many states were seduced by the gaming industry into running government lotteries in the name of "education," preying on the weakest members of society and undermining the American work ethic. Gambling in most states is illegal, and education budgets were not increased but simply shifted, freeing general funds for other spending. Hypocritical politicians abandoned principle to generate revenue, at any cost, to increase government spending.

Americans lived and prospered for 161 years without federal programs to manage our lives. One might argue that people were poor back then; life was harder and less secure, but they were independent and free, with a wealth of pride and dignity. Even Americans shackled by slavery were undaunted in their determination to be free and improve lives for themselves and their families. Has anyone walked through the ghettos of New York or Los Angeles recently? Are these Americans wealthy in property or spirit? Are their lives easy? Do the gangs and guns make them feel secure? Federal programs over the past seventy-two years have done nothing to improve the lives and opportunities for millions of the poorest Americans and never will.

In the pre-Civil War labor debate, slave owners claimed that they provided more security through a lifetime of food and shelter than the sweatshops in the north in which a living could hardly be made and a much less a sense of security felt. What has the U.S. government been doing for seventy years but undermining state, local, and individual responsibilities by implementing massive social programs that it uses to firmly retain control over broad segments of the population? The Thirteenth Amendment made slavery unconstitutional, but the government created a new type of slavery, enforced with the shackles of dependence, to advance and perpetuate the interest of the government and those politicians that hold power. The more those Americans are dependent, the heavier the shackles.

The American government's budget deficits began to grow steadily in the 1980s while at the same time financial institutions were deregulated. In the 1990s, regulation and mandates encouraged industries to ignore market forces and trends. These actions have led to companies "too large to be allowed to fail" and government bailouts and ownership. For those shocked by the federal bailout of 2009 and bankruptcy of General Motors, that company's demise is no different from that of the federal government that has been bailed out by foreign loans, dragged down by unsustainable entitlements, and faced with inevitable national bankruptcy. No entity is too large or too small to fail.

Companies are no less susceptible to the nature of man than governments. Members of a management team or corporate board's shared responsibility creates a greater challenge to personal character and actions in the best interest of the stockholders California is generally considered a window into the future of the nation. Today California has a deficit equal to 25 percent of the State budget; government programs people have come to depend on are now being slashed. Is there anyone who believes that this does not foreshadow catastrophe for the nation?

A government of individuals of character and virtue is likely to be a good government. Voters who hold those representatives accountable and diminish temptation and stagnation by limiting their service are good and responsible citizens.

The challenge for Americans, individually and collectively, is to have the courage to guard government against our natural weaknesses: selfishness, hubris and avarice. A government that promotes the best nature of man through a stable and secure society without unnecessarily encroaching upon individual freedoms is one that best serves the needs of all.

Principles of Republican Government

A *CONSTITUTIONAL* republic is the most effective form of government in which men may pursue life, liberty, and happiness.

Liberalism was founded on the idea that human nature is characterized by reason and tolerance. John Locke's recognition of "the self" led to the modern understanding of identity and the relationship between the individual and social order.

Locke had profound influence on philosophers of the eighteenth century and consequently the thinking and beliefs of the founding gathers. Liberalism stressed human rationality, individual property, natural rights, protection of civil liberties, free markets, and limitations on government. Power was in the hands of the people, and democracy was the logical basis for governance. These concepts consumed the thinking of the founding fathers and are the basis upon which the Declaration of Independence and the Constitution were conceived and written. In his book *Political Ideology Today*, Ian Adams explains that if a free and open social order was established and government got out of the way, human nature and natural forces would lead to the benefit of all of society.

Constitutional governments are autonomous political entities established by written document with specific and limited powers. A democracy is a government charged with executing the will of the majority of the people with consideration for the minority. Because the size of a true democracy is limited, a republican government allows the will of the people to be exercised on a larger scale through representation.

Governments that espouse different purposes such as collectivism have a broader definition of the purpose of government. Collectivism elevates collective interests above individual free will. As one moves along the spectrum from anarchy to totalitarianism, freedom is sacrificed to chaos at one extreme and to oppression at the other. A constitutional, democratic republic moving toward collectivism is one in which the people give up freedoms in exchange for more government structure and control. Because the powers of government are limited and defined in the Constitution (U.S. Constitution, art. 1, sec. 8), ideological movement within the government and its function is limited and can be empowered to expand only by constitutional amendment.

The Treaty of Paris (1783) marked the end of the Revolutionary War. It was not between the British government and the United States, because the United States did not have a government but a confederation. The treaty was between the British government and "Acknowledging the Thirteen Colonies to be free, sovereign, and independent States," which each state ratified separately.

The founding fathers were faced with the challenge of determining how thirteen sovereign States would relate to and support each other while preserving the concepts of individualism and freedom. Further, they needed to balance the divine rights recognized in the Declaration with civil authority to make laws. The Constitution succeeded in fulfilling the promise of the Declaration and the need for civil authority.

Those who are governed expect those who rule, who have the greatest impact on their society and lives, to possess certain virtues. Virtues become important because the people must have faith that those elected are guided by principles and have the courage to act in the best interest of those governed. Character in politicians is imperative for a government to be representative and effective.

Elections favor the rich, influential, and popular, which subjects the process of determining leadership roles to corruption and inequality of influence among citizens. American citizens are equal in that they have the right to vote and may participate in the recruitment, campaign, and election of representatives they feel will best serve their interests. However, many people interested in running for elective office are, or want to be, influential and popular, and they are often able to run for office because they have the means or have the support of wealthy special interests. Today, money drives elections, and therefore our government is formed and undemocratically influenced by wealthy individuals and corporations. Congress recognizes this flaw and has struggled to solve the problem of the influence of money in government. This problem has been grossly complicated by Supreme Court rulings that "money equals free speech" and corporations have the same rights as individuals. These opinions are flawed, because free speech is not the right to be heard, and corporations are not endowed with unalienable divine rights (although, like citizens, corporations should enjoy reasonable protections from government persecution defined by legislation).

The opinions of the majority of Americans are not accurately reflected by the media or outcomes of elections, because extreme positions and biases dominate the news and campaigns. Controversy sells advertising, which wins elections. The media and science of marketing, driven by money disproportionately raised by wealthy individuals, corporations, and special interests creates undue influence. Even within an organization like the American Association of Retired Persons (AARP) or unions, millions of members pay dues and a handful of executives make decisions on spending millions of dollars to support candidates on single issues that may or may not reflect the positions of many if not most of its members. New forms of media have mitigated this imbalance in advertising to some degree. However, social media is complicated and inundating and lacks the focus to drive campaigns.

By limiting political donations to eligible voters and levels within the reach of most Americans, say $100, elections would be more democratic and driven by merit, making it easier for the people to understand the real issues and positions and hold politicians accountable for their records. By ruling money to be equal to speech and corporations equal to a person, the Supreme Court has unjustly subordinated the right of power to minority and special interest groups. Americans know that many who run for elective office for noble reasons often, once in office, are influenced by the political system contrary to the interests of their constituents. The people must be allowed to participate in a reasoned discussion of merits and records free of the shrill hysteria of overwhelming and negative campaigns.

Virtues discussed in ancient Greece by Socrates and Plato necessary for the proper behavior of the Athenian *polis* were adopted by cultures and religions over the centuries to define man's relationships with man, God, and the State.

Ancient understanding of civic virtue was not simply the right to participate in the political process but the expectation that it was the citizen's duty to put his individual interests aside to serve the State. During the European Renaissance, the concept of civic virtue became grounded in the desire to educate to promote good over sinful behavior. Civic conversation encouraged listening, coming to agreement, and staying informed. Civilized behavior required both physical and emotional discipline. Work was a recognized civic virtue, because every person was expected to contribute to society.

The republican revolutions of the eighteenth century redefined civic virtue based on the belief and popularity of freedom. The monarchies or ruling elite looked down on the working class that lived in abject poverty. The expansion in travel and trade gave rise to a new, wealthy merchant class. Landless people who had migrated from the fields to the cities were encouraged to work to contribute to society. However, this led to less tolerance for the class of nonworking elite, establishing a moral imperative for relative opportunity and wealth even in a free society. Education again became the emphasis for civic responsibility to lower the barriers that kept the masses in a state of poverty and oppression. The people had to be educated to improve their lot in life and to achieve freedom. As opposed to a monarchy or ruling class that could order the people to serve, republics were required to persuade the people to subordinate their interests to that of the State. This could be achieved only if the people believed the State or the government could provide an environment in which they could improve their condition.

At the time of the American Revolution, public service was widely considered a civic responsibility. It was believed that service should be provided without compensation. Independent means ensured that self-interest was not pursued while in office. The Victorian period saw a return to parental authority in the family as well as the State. Social reforms sought to define individual behavior and then targeted groups of people driven by a consciousness of oppression in society. Movements in the early twentieth century sought to eliminate classes by encouraging class cooperation over class struggle.

Eligibility to vote in the United States (U.S. Constitution, amend. 15, 19, 24, and 26,) has expanded throughout our history to include all non-felonious citizens eighteen years of age and older. Voting is a privilege, and to have value, it must require effort. The social contract of citizenship requires voters to be informed. A vote that requires no effort is one without value and will be exercised only by those with nothing to lose and everything to gain. Unlimited voting with no requirements rewards irresponsibility and diminishes the purpose and value of the vote. It therefore is the denial of freedom. Those from which nothing is required to vote are susceptible to influence from unscrupulous politicians and special interests. At the same time, unreasonable obstacles have the same destructive effects. To retain value and purpose in support of an effective government, requirements for voting must be carefully balanced against reasonable access to the ballot box.

The federal government was established parallel to state governments, not superior to them, and for the purpose of representing the common interests of the multiple states. State governments, however, represent the people. Requiring all decisions to pass through state legislatures to the federal government removed the individual one step from the democratic process. Although some federal positions are filled by state legislatures or temporary appointments by the governor, today the legislative and executive branches for both federal and state governments are elected directly by the people. Although the Civil War established that States cannot secede from the Union unilaterally, and greatly increased federal power, it did not change the organization and relationship of our government. The Tenth Amendment states, "The powers not delegated to the United States by the Constitution, nor prohibited by it to the States, are reserved to the States respectively, or to the people." The federal government has specific and limited powers, while the State and local governments retain an unlimited list of all other powers. Republican government is the best form of government in a free society. However, in the United States, the greatest difficulty we face as a nation is not the form of government but the conflict between the responsibilities and powers of the federal and state governments.

If power resides with each individual, the most democratic and effective government is one in which decisions are pushed down to the lowest common denominator. Each individual is responsible for himself while the preponderance of governmental authority and responsibility rests at the State level. Federal usurpation of state authority is not only unconstitutional but adverse to republican principles. An ideal democratic republic is one in which the federal and state governments restrict their exercise of power to those defined by their constitutions, allowing the majority of decisions and legislation to be decided at the local level with support from superior governments but free of mandates. Laws that attempt to standardize beliefs or behaviors across the nation are undemocratic and deny local communities the right to govern themselves.

As we have established, in a free society there cannot be equality of ability or property, but members of the smallest homogenous group do have an equal ability to determine who among them may best exercise the interests of the whole. Over our nation's history, Americans have come to acknowledge the stake every person has in government. More importantly, regardless of ability or property, free-thinking citizens possess common sense that cumulatively reflects the collective wisdom of the people. The closer decisions are made to the local level, the less influenced those decisions will be by factions or special interests. Therefore, they are most likely to represent the desires of the majority in that community and the nation.

The establishment, growth, and success of the United

States, and therefore the concept of self-government, are grounded in the willingness to compromise. Compromise produced an imperfect Constitution but one broad enough to allow the necessary flexibility and specific powers for amending or abolishing. Compromise softens the edges of specific interests and arguments, promoting opportunities for success. When citizens, states, and nations have been willing to compromise to achieve collective interests, the nation has flourished. Extreme positions harden against the promise of compromise, test constitutionality, and threaten self-government.

If we favor supporting the efforts of those less fortunate among us, ensuring security and peace, government reflecting the interests of the majority with consideration for minority and stable employment growth, hopefullymost Americans would agree. The question is how to create these conditions and, if we disagree on the method, how to compromise.

When everything gravitates to a national level, we are looking for common ground between over three hundred million people who live across a vast region with substantial differences in geography, culture, and tradition. This is much more difficult than deciding within a single community, town, or county how sex education should be taught in the schools. A national mandate on curriculum will cause enormous conflicts in all parts of the nation, while local decisions reflect a more homogenous view primarily affected by local culture and tradition, which can be quickly changed if necessary. By the same token, the agendas of special interest groups attempt to impose beliefs on local behavior. Extreme civil rights groups routinely recruit individuals in local communities to challenge tradition in the name of civil liberties. A small, Christian community with a volunteer fire department that traditionally builds a nativity scene in front of the firehouse is not violating anyone's civil rights or the separation of church and state. For outside groups to recruit one person, whether non-Christian, agnostic, or atheist, to challenge this practice is to allow one person to veto the desire and tradition of the majority of the community. This is a grotesque perversion of the tenet that "Congress shall make no law respecting an establishment of religion." By interpreting a nativity scene at a firehouse as a violation of one person's rights, the courts have ruled that one person's right not to be exposed to a Christian display is greater than the rights of all members of that community combined undermines democratic principles and practices. The First Amendment was never intended in any form, definition, or interpretation to subvert democratic government and self-rule but applies especially within a small, largely homogenous community.

Special interest groups have also perverted expected conversation in polite society into political correctness. Political correctness supresses speech and is the antithesis of the inherent right to speak in a free society by asserting pressure in favor of specific political ideologies or beliefs.

If the people want more government in their lives, the Constitution gives them the power to pass amendments to extend additional powers to the federal government. For the federal government to unilaterally expand its powers and disregard the intent of the Constitution is to render the Constitution invalid — and therefore the government it creates.

Recognition of a divine power and the willingness to compromise are critical elements of a good government. Equal participation and influence by eligible voters will ensure the election of virtuous individuals with strong character who are most likely to demonstrate courage in the operation of government and who more closely reflect their constituents. An engaged, hard-working citizenry drives a nation's prosperity.

A republican government must constantly balance opposing forces in government and society: Constitutional versus legislative power, voter responsibility versus corruption and undue influence, rules of government that provide equal opportunity and encourage relative affluence, social justice in an evolving society versus equal justice, civil rights versus majority rule; federal versus state authority and responsibility.

A constitutional, republican government established by an informed electorate, responsibly exercising their vote, maintains balance in the execution of duties and effectively protects against abuses, inequality, and injustice. A good and effective constitutional republican government promotes the greatest opportunities for all.

Powers and Rights

*T*HE limited powers of the federal government and individual rights are defined in the Constitution. Dilution or selective application of the Constitution weakens and exposes the nation's vulnerabilities. Abandonment of the Constitution (and, consequently, the dissolution of the nation) would deny all Americans entitlements, protections, and freedom.

Abraham Lincoln stated in 1858 that "a house divided against itself cannot stand." He was speaking about the country being divided between free and slave states, but today that statement applies to ideological extremes.

Extreme partisanship has come to characterize our major national political parties while we simultaneously witness the dissolution of our national bedrock. We read in

Matthew 7:24–27, "Everyone then who hears these words of mine and does them will be like a wise man who built his house on the rock. And the rain fell, and the floods came, and the winds blew and beat on that house, but it did not fall, because it had been founded on the rock. And everyone who hears these words of mine and does not do them will be like a foolish man who built his house on the sand. And the rain fell, and the floods came, and the winds blew and beat against that house, and it fell, and great was the fall of it." The Constitution of the United States is the rock upon which this nation stands, but the courts have eroded the rock, turning it into sand.

The limits on the interpretation of the Constitution are guided by the principles that the Constitution establishes as the supreme law of the land (U.S. Constitution, art. 6). When a situation arises when limitations of powers in the Constitution limit the interpretation of constitutionality pertaining to a specific case and when the people are dissatisfied with the limited interpretation, they are empowered by the Constitution to make appropriate changes in the form of amendments (U.S. Constitution, art. 5). The bar for amending the Constitution is set very high, because the Constitution has the specific purpose of defining the government, powers, and principles of the nation. It is not an instrument to be used at the whim of the courts and politicians. The bedrock of principles upon which the nation stands should not be easily changed. Congress is the institution designed to sway, through legislation, with the changing needs of the people and the political climate.

A perfect example of the failure to implement these roles as intended is the ratification (1919) and subsequent repeal (1933) of the Eighteenth Amendment. Abolition of the "manufacture, sale, or transportation of intoxicating liquors" was not a principle deserving to be part of the Constitution, but clearly it represented commerce subject to legislation. Congress is empowered to regulate interstate commerce and could have easily taxed the interstate distribution of alcohol out of existence. Daniel Webster argued in McCullough v. Maryland (1819), "An unlimited power to tax involves, necessarily, the power to destroy." By using federal legislation through the power to regulate interstate commerce rather than a constitutional amendment, it would have been left to the states to determine whether or not alcohol could be produced and sold within state lines. Raising this issue to the point of a constitutional amendment was an ill-advised attempt to control commerce within the states and to deny individual free will. Its' passage was inconsistent with the purpose and function of the Constitution and was ultimately rejected by the States.

The Constitution states, "The judicial Power shall extend to all Cases, in Law or Equity" (U.S. Constitution, art. 3). The Constitution was based on English Common Law. As a result, the Supreme Court often looks to Common Law for clarity or precedence in cases before the court.

When a party to a case before a Common Law court was dissatisfied, the party could appeal to the King or ask for the mercy of the King's court. These cases were delegated to the King's Chancellery and were an appeal for an equitable resolution to a disagreement between private parties. They were a request for a judgment on what was fair. In these cases, the Chancellery was not making a judgment based on established law but on what he thought was a reasonable solution.

These "cases in law" are rulings that determine whether an existing law has been violated. "Cases in equity," or civil cases, prompt rulings to determine what is fair between two parties. The federal judicial system includes jurisdiction over both common and equity law and by combining the characteristics of these separate types of law in considering cases before a court. Federal judges make rulings based not on violation or constitutionality of the law but on whether the judge rules the law is "fair." This process has greatly expanded the power of the judiciary and has enabled a minority to wield power through the courts over the interests of the majority.

During the 2002 election, a New Jersey senatorial candidate facing corruption charges was replaced at the last minute, but the deadline for filing as a candidate had long passed and the ballots were printed. The New Jersey Supreme Court ruled that all ballots must be reprinted with the new candidate's name, because the date for the deadline was arbitrary and not to do so would be unfair. If one date is arbitrary, why aren't all dates arbitrary except in the case of historical events? Does this mean that legislatures cannot use dates in making law, or that the law may be dismissed at any time by a judge because dates are arbitrary?

The New Jersey legislature established laws for registering as a candidate with requirements including deadlines, because ballots needed to be prepared and the election date was set. The court dismissed the law, and the result was the determining factor in the balance of power in the Senate. The courts undermined the democratic process and the will of the people as reflected through their elected representatives.

Why would courts in a democracy allow an individual or an organization to choose, on its own initiative and interest, to claim to represent the "interests of the people" better than the government that the people elected? By allowing third parties to sue in the name of the public interest, the courts have allowed interference with the government that acts on behalf of the majority of the people, eroding democratic principles.

The greatest challenge for Americans today is not whether Social Security checks will materialize upon retirement but whether the Constitution has been shredded and rendered moot through disregard. The Constitution must be clarified and relegitimized for Americans to achieve our common goals and continue to prosper. Otherwise, our nation is threatened by continued, increasingly venomous divisions across cultural and ideological lines, which result in the slow strangulation of our republic. Congressional contempt for limited government powers, and individual demand for rights to unrestrained behavior, must be checked to preserve the stability and prosperity of our society.

The founding fathers provided much pliability in the Constitution to allow for flexible application and amendment. When interpretation changes the meaning of words in the Constitution, the document has in essence been amended. Article V specifically reserves the power to amend the Constitution through the states by ratification of three-fourths of the legislatures. Judicial interpretations that change the meaning and application of the Constitution are in and of themselves unconstitutional and contrary to what the founding fathers envisioned or intended.

Constitutional interpretation exists only when a law or action is challenged in the courts. Judges interpret the Constitution based on standards of jurisprudence. A Constitution consisting of limited powers is subject to limited interpretation. If the meaning of the powers intended to be given to the government by the Constitution is changed, the definition of power has changed, and therefore the Constitution itself has changed.

This possibility was addressed in the opinion of Marbury v. Madison (1803): "The powers of the legislature are defined and limited; and that those limits may not be mistaken or forgotten, the constitution is written. To what purpose are powers limited, and to what purpose is that limitation committed to writing; if these limits may, at any time, be passed by those intended to be restrained?"

Is the power to interpret the Constitution a power enumerated to the judicial branch of the government? It is not. The Supreme Court granted itself the power in the opinion for Marbury v. Madison: "It is emphatically the province and duty of the judicial department to say what the law is . . . So if a law be in opposition to the Constitution: if both the law and the Constitution apply to a particular case, so that the court must either decide that case conformably to the law, disregarding the Constitution; or conformably to the Constitution, disregarding the law: the court must determine which of these conflicting rules governs the case. This is of the very essence of judicial duty. If then the courts are to regard the Constitution; and the Constitution is superior to any ordinary act of the legislature; the Constitution, and not such ordinary act, must govern the case to which they both apply."

The legal establishment came to accept the Supreme Court's authority of judicial review. However, in 222 years, the people have failed to endorse this judicial power through an amendment. Any judicial interpretation that is inconsistent with the principles established by the Constitution, through change in the meaning or definition of words, is abhorrent to the Constitution and therefore void. Detaching specific phrases in the Constitution such as, "provide for the...general Welfare," (U.S. Constitution, art. I, sec. 8) or, "necessary and proper," from the enumerated powers to which they are clearly meant to apply is an abuse of the practice of judicial review. By using these phrases independently of the enumerated powers, the Constitution becomes a document with unlimited powers, which defeats the purpose of a constitutional government by definition and intent.

From the opinion of Gibbons v. Ogden (1824): "In the last of the enumerated powers, that which grants expressly the means for carrying all others into execution, Congress is authorized 'to make all laws which shall be necessary and proper' for the purpose . . . If they contend only against that enlarged construction, which would extend words beyond their natural and obvious import, we might question the application of the term, but should not controvert the principle. If they contend for that narrow construction which, in support or some theory not to be found in the Constitution, would deny to the government those powers which the words of the grant, as usually understood, import, and which are consistent with the general views and objects of the instrument."

Twenty-one years earlier in Marbury v. Madison, "Thus, the particular phraseology of the Constitution of the United States confirms and strengthens the principle, supposed to be essential to all written constitutions, that a law repugnant to the Constitution is void, and that courts, as well as other departments, are bound by that instrument." The opinion continues, "As men whose intentions require no concealment generally employ the words which most directly and aptly express the ideas they intend to convey, the enlightened patriots who framed our Constitution, and the people who adopted it, must be understood to have employed words in their natural sense, and to have intended what they have said. If, from the imperfection of human language, there should be serious doubts respecting the extent of any given power, it is a well settled rule that the objects for which it was given, especially when those objects are expressed in the instrument itself, should have great influence in the construction." The U.S. Constitution, (art. 1, sec. 8) is the object of the words used to describe the application of government powers.

The U.S. Constitution, (art. 6), reads, "This Constitution, and the Laws of the United States . . . shall be the supreme Law of the Land; and the Judges in every State shall be bound thereby." The Constitution clearly gives power to the people, but the authority of judicial review assumed by the Supreme Court changed that dynamic without the necessary checks or balances. The trend toward activism by the courts over the last seventy years has exposed this weakness in the application of the Constitution, thereby undermining our democratic principles and the balance of power.

Man possesses free will and therefore, in a vacuum, an infinite number of inherent rights. Citizens in a society voluntarily subordinate some inherent rights so that laws may be created by the government to serve the interests of the larger community. The Declaration of Independence recognizes the divine rights of the people that the government cannot guarantee but the government can promote an environment in which these rights may best be pursued and enjoyed.

Constitutional rights are those specific protections that the government may not restrict by legislation or persecution. Only the government can violate Constitutional rights, because individuals are not empowered to make law, quarter troops, issue warrants, indict, conduct trials, set bail, punish, or restrict voting. Anything an individual might do that appears to violate someone's rights is not a constitutional violation but a violation of the law or of an inherent right. Rights cannot be products or services, because in a free society, the government's role is not "to make estates" but to create an environment in which citizens may better their condition. Healthcare is not a right and never can be, although in a moral society, relative treatment should be available to those willing to help themselves. Providing healthcare incurs expenses. If people have a right to healthcare provided by the government, the government needs to tax to raise that revenue. Taxes are a taking of freedom from some citizens to provide a material benefit to other citizens. In a free society with equal rights, this condition cannot exist. Social Security, Medicare/Medicaid and worker's compensation pose similar conflicts. However, these are not rights but privileges, and revenues to provide these benefits are raised specifically through payroll, matched by employers, and available to all. Nonetheless, the power to consider legislation creating these entitlements does not exist anywhere in the Constitution, and Social Security was ruled constitutional in 1937 only after continually being ruled unconstitutional with the impasse broken through political pressure.

Constitutional rights are not absolute. Individuals cannot claim rights that overrule the authority of an institution, because freedom is not the right to do what you wish, when or how. Can an individual attending the president's State of the Union Address stand up and begin shouting down the president because of his right to free speech? Preventing or removing a heckler from the Capitol does not violate the heckler's right of free speech, because that person has an infinite number of places and means for expressing his opinion. If free speech were the right to be heard, every person could demand his opinion be printed or broadcast. By the same token, no one has a right to speak freely in a courtroom or a schoolroom, because these institutions require rules and an overriding authority to ensure order.

There is a clear distinction between the constitutional right to free speech (U.S. Constitution, amend. I) and the inherent right to speak in a free society. In the first case, an individual cannot be persecuted for speaking out against the government; however, that individual does not have a right to be heard in all circumstances. In the second case, an individual's ability to speak, or act out, is subject to laws as defined by the legislature or rules by institutional authority. What is not constitutional free speech? Expression is not free speech. Creating art or burning the American flag is not constitutional free speech. If they were, there is literally nothing that could be restrained by law to maintain order. Anything could be considered an expression of what an individual thinks or feels and claimed to be exempt from legislation.

Burning the American flag is abhorrent to the vast majority of Americans. A law restricting defilement of the flag does not prevent an individual from protesting against the government but protects the symbol that represents all that Americans have fought to establish and preserve for over two hundred years. An individual's right to protest against the government in one specific way cannot overrule the interests of the majority to protect the dignity of a national symbol. In the unanimous opinion of Schenck v. United States (1919), Oliver Wendell Holmes, Jr. wrote, "The question in every case is whether the words (this case concerned distribution of pro-Communism brochures but here equally applies to burning the flag) used are used in such circumstances and are of such a nature as to create a clear and present danger that they will bring about the substantive evils (anti-American sentiment) that the United States Congress has a right to prevent. Freedom of speech does not protect an individual from words or actions that might promote anti-American activity or aggravate public sentiment, especially when Americans are at war—which seems to be a perpetual state.

Even more unreasonable is the idea that pornography is free speech because it has nothing to do with protesting against the government and everything to do with degradation, abuse and perversion. It has no redeeming value to society. The court ruled in Butler v. Michigan (1957) that the government cannot, "reduce the adult population . . . to reading only what is fit for children," but the government should be able to limit distribution and exposure of these materials. In Miller v. California (1973), the court established that local communities could restrict what they considered to be materials appealing to "prurient interest" with no redeeming value. However, the Internet has erased the ability to establish and enforce this barrier; therefore, the government should restrict or block obscene Internet content through their power to regulate interstate commerce. This would not prevent those adults who wish to view pornography from producing and distributing it within a state (which state legislatures could address) or privately. The government's ability to act in the interest of the majority has been obstructed by First Amendment claims concerning these issues. The result is a society permeated with the most obscene and immoral images, in many cases illegal acts, that are pervasive through networks at schools, libraries, and even cellphones.

The First Amendment states, "Congress shall make no law respecting an establishment of religion." Religion is an organized approach to spirituality with symbols, rituals, and specific practices. Recognition of God is a reflection of spirituality but is not religion. The Constitution does not restrict the recognition of God, and the minority does not have a right to eliminate God from public institutions. If recognition of God is synonymous with religion, the First Amendment contradicts the Declaration and the Constitution.

The Fourteenth Amendment guarantees "equal protection under the law." Equal rights reflect the growth of the country from its founding to continually strive for the ideal established in the Declaration that "all men are created equal." However, the Fourteenth Amendment applies only to federal and state governments making law, not to businesses or individuals. Again, the courts have expanded the application of the Constitution to broader segments of society, and in doing so have denied business owners and individuals from exercising free will in the daily course of their lives. No person can be coerced into behaving a certain way toward others, because rights and laws cannot be applied inequitably. Persons in a free society have as much right to hate as they do to love. The responsibility falls to society to encourage civil, enlightened behavior.

Because all Americans have not been treated equitably throughout our history by law or society, civil rights emerged as a basis for broad initiatives. Racial preferences are clearly unconstitutional, but our society has deemed them a moral imperative because of our belief in equal opportunity and relative affluence. As we continue as a nation to move toward the ideals of the Declaration, this temporary period of racial preferences, contradictory to the Fourteenth Amendment, is necessary to give all segments of the population the opportunity to improve their condition. In the decades ahead, racial preference will be phased out, and history will appreciate the nation's commitment to our evolving moral standards and the integrity of our ideals.

The courts are responsible for the coarsening of American culture by allowing unrestricted pursuit of profit regardless of the harm to society. By continuing to bring clearly inherent rights under the protection of the Constitution, the courts have created confusion and tied the hands of government to legislate in the interests of the majority to ensure a secure and stable society. The check on legislative abuse is not to be achieved by the courts, forever expanding the definition of constitutional rights, but by citizens through their votes. By defining inherent rights as constitutional rights, the Supreme Court continually blurs the lines of constitutionality, restricts the authority of the government to pass laws to reflect the interests of the majority, and therefore diminishes rights in a democracy. The Constitution cannot be used to elevate an individual's rights over the interests of the majority of the people and the welfare of the nation. Freedom is not the right to do anything you wish, at any time or anywhere.

The people of the United States possess the power of the nation, the constitutional rights to protect against government persecution, and the inherent rights of a free society. The different types of powers and rights are clearly distinguishable but today are subverted to undermine the will of the people. We are again in the midst of a desperate civil war that is ideological and less bloody but no less tragic.

Dangers of Self-Fulfilling Government

A *SOCIETY* in which government is allowed to become an end in itself is not a democracy or a protector of liberty but rather a society in transition toward socialism and communism.

The nature of man is self-interest, and a virtuous life is difficult to achieve and only by the most disciplined of men. Benjamin Franklin argued, "There are two passions which have a powerful influence on the affairs of men. These are ambition and avarice . . . when united in view of the same object they have in many minds the most violent effects."

The people of the United States have allowed the entrenchment of a permanent political class. Career politicians no longer live in their elected communities but in the artificial environment of Washington, DC in which their judgment is shaded, distancing them from the people they represent and subjecting them to continuous and unimaginable temptations. They become imprisoned by their commitments and rigid in their thinking. Franklin continues to define the person attracted to this type environment by saying, "It will not be the wise and moderate; the lovers of peace and good order, the men fittest for the trust. It will be the bold and the violent, the men of strong passions and indefatigable activity in their selfish pursuits."

Even those with the best of intentions are continually challenged. A group is more easily swayed from the straight and narrow when responsibility is spread among all members of the group. James Madison explains, "Respect for character is always diminished in proportion to the number among whom the blame or praise is to be divided. Conscience, the only remaining tie, is known to be inadequate in individuals: In large numbers, little is to be expected from it."

Once a government's institutions become an end in themselves, the liberties of the people are soon eroded. How has this happened in America? How have we allowed the federal government to consolidate such extensive powers and debt? A budget that is not built on costs but on spending is not a budget at all but a license to incur debt. Do Americans really believe that the national debt will not have to be repaid; that the 30 percent deficit spending that adds to our national debt each year is the best use for our tax dollars; that the expenditure of monies that created the debt eradicate poverty, threats, or inequality? The debt has been created for one reason: to perpetuate the office and power of an elite class of professional politicians at the expense of our freedom.

Aristophanes stated, "To plunder, to lie, to show your arse, are three essentials for climbing high." George Washington did not receive a salary as president and went to great effort to ensure that his independent means were known. This was expected of politicians at the time as a demonstration of political integrity and to guard against using government to promote self-interests. When Dwight D. Eisenhower left the presidency in 1961, he got in his car with his wife, Mamie, and drove home. Over the past thirty years, presidents, congressmen, and senators have turned tradition on its head by increasingly using their positions as stepping stones to wealth.

Americans have allowed politicians to enrich themselves through lifelong careers, and in doing so, we have allowed Franklin's fear to be realized: the uniting of ambition and avarice. Mark Twain said in 1894, "It could probably be shown by facts and figures that there is no distinctly American criminal class except Congress." The greatest threat to Americans today is not a tyrannical government but professional politicians.

To represent the people, elected individuals must know, be connected to, and understand the needs and desires of those they represent. Nations fail when strife among factions in the citizenry outweighs common national bonds and when the self-interest of an elected official exceeds the common bond with those represented. When national interests are subordinated to ideology, politics, and party, the politician can no longer effectively serve constituents or the nation. Perpetuating a position in office has become the primary goal of American politicians and the special interests that support them. Those who claim party control, or that their seniority is too great to lose, are saying that they believe the power they have accumulated is more important than broader representation, fresh ideas, and effectiveness.

Many politicians claim experience and knowledge as the reason to remain in office. Government employees— civil servants—are the repository of knowledge that preserve the tradition and operation of our government and institutions. Politicians are expendable.

A government consisting of self-interested politicians is a government of self-interest; politicians interested only in preserving their positions of power form a government interested only in promoting its own interests and expanding its power. No matter how virtuous they may appear during campaigns, these politicians expose their character once in office and shrink before the challenges that require courage.

The history of the United States consists of three distinct periods: 1787 to 1865 represented expansion and maturity; from 1865 to 1945, the nation rose through an industrial and manufacturing economic base to world power; and from 1945 to the present, the United States has projected power and culture worldwide, promoting economic growth, freedom, and peace for all people. However, we have reached a fork in the road for determining the next chapter in our nation's history. All Americans must understand this fork and determine which path we should choose to pursue as a nation and a people.

The Constitution, written in 1787, is a legal contract between the States, and it marked the beginning of the organization of our federal government. As soon as it was ratified, a great debate began over its meaning and application. The most prevalent argument was whether the Constitution consisted of implied powers that allowed Congress to exercise powers not explicitly enumerated in the Constitution but were "necessary and proper" in order to execute those powers. John Marshall served as Chief Justice of the Supreme Court from 1801 until his death in 1835. During that time, he led the effort to shape constitutional law and, in doing so, to consolidate power within the court. During this period, the United States fulfilled the goal of "manifest destiny" while the nation struggled with the issue of slavery, left by the founders for the States to resolve themselves. The States did resolve the issue but not as envisioned or intended. Abraham Lincoln looked to the founding fathers for faith and guidance during his presidency, but the last of the original great constitutional debates ended at a cost of six hundred thousand American lives. The Civil War marked the end of innocence for the new nation and set us on a path toward the promise of the Declaration that "all men are created equal."

From 1865 forward, the United States experienced a powerful and growing central government. The late nineteenth and early twentieth centuries saw an Industrial Revolution that changed the world. Structures were put in place that allowed men to become wealthy beyond anything imagined previously. Morgan, Rockefeller, and Ford built dynasties and the industries that would lead the United States to victory in World War II. The banking collapse of 1929 foreshadowed the Great Depression and initiated federal government regulation of the financial system. World War II brought an end to the Depression and lifted the United States to world power.

With the Industrial Revolution came an urban class of working citizens. Population growth and migration drove workers into factories where their labor was cheap and easily replaceable. A working or "proletariat" class drove the mechanisms required by the great new industries that in turn treated employees with contempt and disregard. The social movements at the turn of the twentieth century sought to address these abuses through unions and governments that promoted relative affluence through economic stability. It is logical that the workers who suffered at the hands of growing and abusive industry practices would look to government for help.

Karl Marx provided the theory upon which socialism, or the government control of major industries to ensure economic stability, was based. Marx was convinced that the free market, driven by profit incentive, would forever be in a cycle that would prevent stability in the work force. He believed that government, exercised by an elite political class and intellectual doctrine, would best provide stable economic and employment conditions.

Locke's theory of liberalism was founded on the natural goodness of man, autonomy of the individual, civil and political liberties, and the rule of law with the consent of the governed. Individuals, through the free market, would drive economic growth and individual achievement.

Today, more generally, liberalism means political reform or change. Conservatism means to preserve or restore the traditional order. Nonetheless, these labels as used today are not mutually exclusive, and both are necessary for an evolving free society and stable economy.

In 1776, the founding fathers were considered liberal, even radical. They opposed the traditional or conservative role of the English monarchy and parliament that ruled the colonies. The social movement of the early twentieth century was a liberal movement, or desire for change, even though Marx's social theory conflicted with Locke's liberal definition of individual autonomy and the responsibility that guided the founding fathers. Nonetheless, change was desired and necessary in the United States at that time. The question was should change be promoted at the structural, or constitutional, level of the country or the operational, or legislative, level? Should we change our form of government through the Constitution to address the evolving needs of industry and society and its relationship to man, or should we change the way government operated through legislation? There was support for both approaches, so the stage was set for an ongoing struggle between those who believed in more government control (to provide stability and promote economic parity) and those who believed in the free market system, individual responsibility, and personal achievement.

With the leadership of Woodrow Wilson and Franklin D. Roosevelt, the new American liberalism sought to expand the federal government's role in regulating private industry and addressing the needs of the most disadvantaged in society. These roles were traditionally held by a self-regulating, free enterprise system and local communities through churches, community chests, families, and neighbors. However, new systems were required to meet the needs of an evolving and increasingly urban society

The 1937 Supreme Court ruling making the Social Security Act constitutional was the first salvo in the political struggle. It continues in an effort to balance the stability and familiarity of conservatism, now labeled "classical liberalism," with the growth and improvement necessary in any evolving society through liberalism.

Following World War II, limited political success of the liberal agenda through legislation led to a shift in strategy to judicial activism. While the Marshall court defined the relationships of government, the judiciary has expanded its power in order to actively influence the nature of our society through government over the past forty years. The usurpation by federal judges of the democratic process puts a strain on constitutional integrity. The result is an ever-expanding and self-fulfilling federal government that has implemented unsustainable social programs and expanded its reach into the daily lives of Americans, thereby undermining our independence and responsibility.

Today, *conservatism* means the desire to adhere to the positions of the founding fathers as expressed through the Constitution. *Liberalism* means the desire to expand the size and control of government to effect social change. However, the Constitution limits federal government authority, therefore restricting liberal progress at the federal level. Therein lays the crux of the problem. Liberal success over the past two decades has pushed federal government activity beyond the authority extended by the Constitution, therefore threatening the validity of the Constitution itself.

Following the Reagan presidency, and in response to the rise of the religious right and a decade of conservative policies, there was a power struggle within the liberal establishment between moderates and radicals. The radicals won, and during all four administrations since that time, the accelerating rate in the growth of the federal government has expanded entitlements, allowed illegal immigration to go unchecked, and allowed numerous other violations of constitutional and States' rights. The national government and public discourse can best be characterized as extreme partisanship, inflexibility, false implications, and personal enrichment through public service. Civility is all but nonexistent.

Expansion of federal power is appropriate during times such as war or acute national crisis. Federal government intervention created dramatic and necessary changes during the Civil War, the Great Depression, and the Civil Rights Movement as well as numerous natural disasters. However, expanded powers must be relinquished once the crisis is resolved. It is a consistent characteristic of governments throughout history that once power is obtained, it is never relinquished voluntarily.

Our constitution allows the people to expand or contract government to take any form desired. However, in its current form, the federal government does not have the constitutional authority to act as it has with expanding characteristics of socialism. Today, the federal government controls 51 percent of all healthcare expenditures through Medicaid and Medicare and provides insurance and retirement benefits to 100 percent of Americans through Social Security. When enacted, these programs were shunned by most Americans who viewed them as taking welfare. Like any addiction, the new generation of Americans growing up with entitlements is almost impossible to wean from dependence. These three programs are mismanaged, cannot be sustained, and are bankrupting the country.

Politics weigh heavily on legislation and the execution or enforcement of legislation from one administration to the next. The people elect the government, and therefore, the government should reflect the wants and desires of the people (or at least those who voted). Although each branch of the government cannot operate based on weekly polls, defying the wishes of the citizenry by governing with impunity and ignoring the limits of enumerated powers is a violation of one's oath of office to "preserve, protect, and defend the Constitution of the United States."

When a government becomes self-perpetuating, functions independently of the interests of the people, and enjoys unrestrained powers, that government is no longer a constitutional one. Executive orders have evolved into legislation by decree: the judiciary amends the Constitution by fiat, and Congress engages in usurpation of the power of the states and the people.

The United States is no longer a nation where the power resides with the people but one in which power resides with the federal government to which state governments and individuals are subordinate. This condition cannot exist under our Constitution, and because this condition does exist, our Constitution, and therefore the nation, is at great risk. Today the argument turns not on whether implied powers in the Constitution exist but whether the Constitution is relevant at all. Does the desire for governmental ability to impose social justice outweigh the integrity of the Constitution?

The purpose and goal of an active and informed electorate is to ensure that the federal government is reduced of self-interest. Professional politicians hold office, where their heads and loyalties are easily turned, due only to the abdication of the American citizen to hold those officials accountable.

The choice we face as we stand at this national crossroad is whether to amend the Constitution to drastically and permanently transfer the power of the people to the federal government or to reaffirm the Constitution and force the federal government to contract within constitutional limits, yielding to the rightful authority of the States and the people. Taking no action is by default a vote for invalidating the Constitution, given the direction the nation is moving today. Inaction is an implicit endorsement of the status quo. To take the high road toward constitutional reaffirmation, proper realignment of State and federal powers, and national preservation, the people must actively remove career politicians and the States must proactively seek amendments to curb judicial activism and clarify constitutional validity and intent.

A self-fulfilling government is not a government of the people but one that is dangerously out of control and increasingly moving in the direction of totalitarianism or collapse. Republican government, which reflects the divine nature of man, must be preserved and strengthened so that mankind will benefit from the continued sovereignty and pre-eminence of American leadership.

Civis Americus Sum

*P*ERPETUATION of American liberty is subject to
our individual and collective ability to act in the
best interest of the nation, guided by our common bond as
Americans.

Civis romanus sum was a statement of pride and
privilege in the ancient Roman Empire. *Civis Americus sum,*
("I am an American citizen") is a statement of
responsibility to our founding fathers and the
constitutional government they created, to all who have
fought and died for freedom, and to ourselves and our
children to preserve democracy. We have been handed an
enormous responsibility, as the leaders of the free world,
to influence the course of mankind through these
challenging times. To effectively lead, we must have a

clear understanding of the journey we have traveled as a nation and the direction we wish to pursue

Freedom will not survive for long among men without character, for character is required to sacrifice one's interest for those of others. Freedom must constantly be defended against the encroachment of ambitious men whose egos drive their actions and whose words are carefully crafted for each audience they address. Defense of freedom requires the exposure of charlatans in our government by the calm and steady words of the American people despite the boisterous remonstrations of the parties, press, and special interests. We must each stand strong in the face of fear and danger. The defense of freedom requires courage and fortitude.

To achieve continued improvement in our national life, the collective wisdom of the people must be heard, and the government reduced of self-interest. We must act to perpetuate our prosperity in order to allow subsequent generations the opportunity to do the same. We must embrace those virtues by which our founding fathers measured character and trust. Money alone must cease acting as the driving force behind daily decisions. We must rediscover the joy of serving others and the nation. Our revolution must begin with understanding our journey, followed by civil and reasoned discourse.

The Roman Republic devolved into a despotic empire following the social upheaval that was driven by prosperity. Ancient Britain was slowly conquered by Saxons not by force as much as by internal dissension. Winston Churchill said, "The one thing we have learned from history is that we don't learn from history." Unfortunately, Americans demonstrate once again that excessive prosperity and internal divisiveness are a formula for decline. All things experience cycles, and nations are no exception. The twentieth century British philosopher, Malcolm Muggeridge, prophesized, "It's in the nature of man and of all that he constructs to perish, and it must ever be so." This statement is true, but the people have the ability to affect this outcome for the foreseeable future if they heed the lessons of history and act in our nation's best interest. Americans can change the inevitable by improving the quality of our republic through civic consciousness.

Karl Marx criticized capitalism as a doomed social model. He theorized that capitalism would lead to prosperity, consumerism, and finally debt in a perpetual cycle. America is on the course toward proving Marx correct unless we dramatically change our daily decisions.

An America that continues to operate on deficit spending, subordinates personal decisions to government dictates, and continues to allow increasing control over the private sector by government and corporations unlimited in size and power will cease being the leader of the free world within our lifetimes.

The United States is irresponsibly devaluing the dollar, and national bankruptcy, a real prospect, will result in a devastating worldwide depression and realignment of power among nations.

Most first-generation Americans arrived in this country with nothing. Their dream was for their children to live a better life. People of all races and cultures came to the United States from all over the world, creating new tensions and conflicts with each wave of immigration. As individuals exercised their right to the pursuit of happiness and to improve their condition in life, each generation found better opportunities, and the cultures assimilated. The diverse peoples became Americans with a common interest in national identity.

Following World War II, America reached the pinnacle of power and compassion. Along with her allies, America defeated the Axis threat and invested to rebuild the European communities and economies that were critical to Americas continued economic growth. The 1950s and 1960s witnessed a social enlightenment and saw a movement toward equality with the goal of bringing together all people under the umbrella of freedom and opportunity. Unfortunately, as African-Americans became the most visible beneficiary of this movement, more and more specific groups of Americans began to claim rights and special consideration for their minority status, not for equal treatment. The events have split America into factions that have replaced our sense of national unity with sharply divided, specific, and narrow interests.

We are all products of our environment. With the affluence after World War II, our environment changed, resulting in new generations that demonstrated narcissism and complacency. Today, most Americans do not dream of creating a better life for their children but dream of satisfying personal desires through selfish interests, amenities, or government benefits. Americans' excessive lifestyles and ever-greater consumerism are false manifestations of progress and happiness.

With the rise in scientific discovery in the twentieth century, there has been a decline in religion as the central tenet by which most American's lives are guided. Our nation was founded on divine rights, but today we are losing the basis on which we share common interests and goals. This divisive trend will continue to lead to internal conflict and division, making America weaker and more vulnerable.

The majority of Americans tend to be more conservative on fiscal issues and more liberal on social issues. How can our Constitution be effectively exercised to achieve the interests of all parties? If the federal government were to limit its exercise of power to those enumerated, we would have no federal deficit and would be much less "compassionately" imperialistic in our world view. If all social programs were initiated, funded, and operated at the State level, specific needs could be addressed more efficiently and effectively. Fifty states would pursue programs to meet their citizen's specific needs, and by working together, states would adopt best practices from each other, thereby promoting continual improvement and flexibility. Some would argue that a good program should be rolled out nationally. I would suggest that national programs are difficult to administer, are not adjusted for local and regional needs, and would not allow for the experimentation of a range of approaches that could be easily and quickly adjusted when necessary. The only reason to insist on federalization of social programs is so that a small number of people can control a large number of people. This approach of "a few at the top dictating to the many at the bottom" is contrary to the concepts of democracy, free will, and independence.

Charity begins with the individual and is expressed through community and institutions. Philanthropy in the United States is overwhelmingly the greatest voluntary sharing of resources and assets in history. The federal authority of endowment cannot be found anywhere in the Constitution.

Today, life is more urban and hectic than in generations past. Mobility reduces community and family cohesion and turns our homes into merely houses with equity. Roles and relationships between men and women have changed, and our children bear the burden of our narcissism. Today's prosperity is manufactured. The better life we proclaim for our children requires daily medication to manage anxiety and behavioral syndromes. Only a return to the strength of the family and mutual support within the community will insure a better future for our children and nation, if we chose that to be our goal.

Credit is not economic growth, and debt is not prosperity. When homes become houses that provide credit used to consume, Americans have taken a seriously wrong turn. Mortgages drive house sizes, illegal immigrants provide cheap labor, materials, furniture and fixtures for the new homes that drive the economy, appreciation creates false equity, and Americans borrow to maintain the illusion of prosperity. The demise of the savings and loan industry in the 1980s foreshadowed today's debacle.

We must wean ourselves off credit and begin saving. We must transform our houses back into homes and work toward a well-deserved "mortgage burning" celebration. We need to buy one-year-old cars and keep them well maintained for twice the number of years that it takes to pay them off. We must put money into savings and let it grow for our security and our children's benefit. Americans must reject the idea that we must spend money to support the economy and instead support the nation by buying American.

The American people have accepted a coarsening of our society in the name of unlimited individual freedom and diversity. We have allowed a small but aggressive and vocal minority to redefine freedom as the elimination of social standards while vilifying tradition. It has become vulgar in the eyes of the cultural elite to live and practice Christianity and admirable to spew obscenities and demonstrate a total lack of moral standing. Self-respect has been replaced by a previously unheard-of arrogance demonstrated through prostitution of the mind and body. Diversity is used selectively as a catch phrase for progress and enlightenment, but in practice it undermines advancement, democracy, and demonizes tradition.

Media exists only through our support. The proliferation of editorial news has seeped into mainstream American media and undermined journalistic standards. All forms of media antagonize the public by pitting extremes against one another and promoting sensationalism. American problems and solutions are not black and white; the collective wisdom of the people lies within the spectrum of color where reason and tolerance reside. Americans must reject media hyperbole by changing the station, turning off the television, discontinuing subscriptions, and bypassing newsstands. Americans must reject an ideologically driven media in favor of reason and tolerance.

Collectively we must reassert the authority of the Constitution and better define and enforce the limited powers of the federal government. Defining distinctions between constitutional and inherent rights will provide clear guidance for interpretation and application of laws. Congress should be required to justify authority for legislation by passing the Enumerated Powers Act and employ rules that promote transparency. The people should have confidence in our professional class of civil servants and eliminate professional politicians by imposing term limits. Fiduciary power must be severely restricted, including limitations on national debt and required sunset provisions on all legislation for raising revenue. Congress should not be allowed to exempt its members from legislation or impose mandates on states, much less without funding. American military power must be utilized judiciously and only through the constitutional authority of Congress to declare war. The courts' power of judicial review should be recognized in conjunction with congressional authority to vacate constitutional opinions that violate the authority of the States. Law must be reformed to prevent it being used by a few as a veto over the government that is elected by the majority.

Courage is the quality of spirit that enables man to prosper and live free. America is allowed to carry the torch of freedom and hope for the world today because of the character of brave men twenty-six hundred years ago, their culture of honor, and their willingness to sacrifice their own lives selflessly. The city-states of Athens and Sparta in 480 BC were the seeds of democracy. Although they fought among themselves, the threat of submission and persecution by the invading Persians under Xerxes aligned their interests. The emergence of Greek nationalism tilled the soil from which all Western civilization would grow.

The Greek dramatist Aeschylus recognized that "against [freedom's] strength, no one can fight and win." We must each stand strong in the face of fear and danger. The defense of freedom requires courage.

The North Carolina novelist Thomas Wolfe wrote, "Man's grandeur, tragic dignity, his heroic glory came from the brevity and smallness of this flame [mortality]." The American people are great because they understand that they are part of a much bigger picture in the world and in the future of mankind. As a free nation and people, we choose individually and collectively to stand against threats to ourselves and to freedom around the world, despite danger and criticism.

Sun Tzu, the great Chinese warrior, said, "Divide and conquer." What has been happening in America over the last fifty years? Have we become more united or less? Have special interests become more influential in politics, and therefore our daily lives, or less? Has our "free press" provided clear, honest assessments of our government, or has the press become a pawn of ideology, big business, and special interests? Are Americans standing together and strong against internal dissention and foreign aggression? Have Americans allowed venomous discourse to poison nationalism and the collective mood and create anxiety and anger in our daily lives?

If America is more divided today than in our past, we are more susceptible to external threats, internal dissension, or unconstitutional characteristics of socialism. Once we allow the supersession of our national identity by political, racial, cultural, or moral factions, we will no longer be able to stand as a nation, much less as a world power. Is the idea of freedom and democracy bigger than individuals, factions, or a whole generation? Once the torch of freedom is extinguished, is there anyone who believes it is easily rekindled?

The character of the American people must be preserved, and those with the strongest character must be chosen to represent our interests. Americans must choose courageous individuals to represent them, individuals who will stand against fear, danger, and criticism to protect the individual freedoms that collectively form our national identity. For Americans to allow the ambition of factions to drive a wedge between the people and degrade our freedoms will be to surrender our nation to selfish interests. Like the Greeks almost three millennia ago, Americans must recognize the mutual threat to our nation.

After visiting Mount Vernon while en route to the First Continental Congress in 1774, Virginian delegate Edmund Pendleton described Martha Washington in a letter, "I was much pleased with Mrs. Washington and her spirit. She seemed ready to make any sacrifice and was cheerful though I knew she felt anxious. She talked like a Spartan mother to her son on going to battle. 'I hope you will stand firm—I know George will,' she said."

America needs leaders of spirit willing to sacrifice for the nation. Where are the American Spartans? Where are the brave men and women who will represent our interests and perpetuate freedom for the next century with honesty, sincerity, and purpose? Today, every American must be a Spartan, for only Spartans can keep us free.

Read the limits on federal government authority (U.S. Constitution, art. 1, sec. 8), and ask yourself if the federal government has exceeded its authority and is acting unconstitutionally.

Read the authority reserved for the States and the people (U.S. Constitution, amend. X).

Assess your personal situation, and seek to better align with personal and national interests by downsizing, saving, reconnecting with family, putting your children first, and volunteering.

Become informed and support those judges and candidates with strong character who most closely represent your interests and beliefs.

Reject media sources that are sensational or extremely

biased, radical views and uncivil discourse, and immoral behavior and attacks on traditional values.

Stand up for yourself, your family, and your nation and, as Martha Washington described George Washington's actions, "stand firm."

Just as there are patriotic Americans, there are those who oppose America and the ideals upon which the nation has been built. Political opposition is not to be confused with anti-American sentiment. Political action is the process of working within the Constitution to effect change even to the point of promoting the need for a constitutional convention. Those who ignore, defy, or hold in contempt the Constitution or would undermine liberty or individual freedom, are anti-American by opposing the values upon which America was founded. Those who disregard their responsibility to be informed or to even vote are poor Americans whose apathy is the difference between effective and incompetent governance.

We must seek and elect to public office those men and women of character whose interest begins and ends with service and understand that a regular infusion of new representation, and therefore new ideas and energy, is much more important than an individual's seniority or sense of self-importance.

The need for an American Civic Revolution exists because we have lost the bonds that define us as Americans. We no longer accept our Constitution as a document of principle and guidance, but we view it as a smorgasbord from which we can pick and choose. The meaning and use of the words *freedom, rule of law, democracy,* and *rights* are misunderstood and misapplied in daily word and deed. We were once "all in this together," but today our selfish interests outweigh those of family and nation. It would appear that the poor state of our federal government accurately reflects the personal failings of our society. Continued fractionalization among political, cultural, ethnic, educational, and economic lines cannot be sustained without an overriding national bond. We must return to basics, individually and collectively. We must push to the forefront those values and characteristics the vast majority of Americans share and practice daily. We must demand civility from public and private institutions, public figures, entertainers, coworkers, neighbors, family members, and spouses. We must instill in our children a sense of respect for their elders and themselves. We must open our minds, our ears, and our hearts to compromise. We must exercise civility to rediscover our national bonds and the security those bonds offer for our future.

The American people must elevate our shared identity as a people and a nation over all other interests. Our individual positions on the world, nation, and politics are not necessarily wrong, but we must be willing to consider alternative ways to view the same issues in order to discover common ground.

Perpetuation of American pre-eminence is inextricably tied to a sense of responsibility, which is possible only if American citizens take action. *Civis Americus sum*; we all must accept responsibility, take action in our daily and public lives, and proclaim, "I am an American citizen."

Bill of the People

T *en Amendments to Save America*

I. Judicial Review

The Supreme Court of the United States shall have the power of judicial review. Inferior courts to which the Supreme Court delegates authority are limited to acting on cases within their assigned jurisdiction.

The Constitution does not assign the power of constitutional review to any branch of government. In the first constitutional challenge during the case of Marbury vs. Madison (1803), Thomas Jefferson believed the executive branch should have the authority, but in the opinion by Chief Justice John Marshall, the Supreme Court reasoned that judicial review was logically a function of the judiciary. The Constitution, by definition, does not allow the federal government to expand its own powers, and with the words "judicial review" nowhere to be found in the Constitution, this power is clearly not delegated. Marshall's opinion could only have been achieved by unconstitutionally ignoring the Tenth Amendment, so this power is clearly reserved for the States. Although the Supreme Court awarded itself the power of judicial review and that authority has been generally recognized by the legal community since the decision in 1803, this delegation of power to the judiciary has never been constitutionally verified in the form of an amendment. This power needs to be recognized as that of the judiciary but only in conjunction with further checks and balances to guard against the politicization of court appointments, judicial activism that encroaches on the powers and responsibilities of the States, and the erosion of constitutional integrity.

Congress has the power of creating inferior federal courts. With advancements in travel and communications, judicial activism has become more prevalent. Plaintiffs have searched the country for federal judges who may make a ruling in their favor regardless of the issue or the location where the suit originated. This practice has weakened our democracy and undermines the integrity of the judiciary. The Supreme Court and Congress have failed to correct this practice by establishing appropriate rules for jurisdiction of these inferior courts. This failure of action and the consequential erosion of democracy requires the people to correct this practice by limiting the jurisdiction of federal judges.

II. Senate Oversight of Constitutional Review

The Senate may determine if federal court rulings are of constitutional significance and elect to review those opinions. By a vote of two-thirds of its members the Senate may vacate the court's decision and by doing so identify the issue as one reserved to the States or if the ruling is desired but outside of the authority of the Constitution the Senate may initiate a constitutional amendment for consideration by the States.

Despite our belief in an independent judiciary, constitutional opinions are often influenced by politics and social trends. From Dred Scott vs. Sanford (1857) to Roe vs.

Wade (1973), we see this happening. In addition to this inevitable practice, and with the politicization of the Supreme Court nominating process by the Senate in considering Reagan-nominee Robert Bork for the court in 1987, the Court's independence, impartiality, and commitment to intellectual legal scholarship has been further undermined. Although the Senate is a political body itself, by vacating a court decision, the Senate has not made a ruling on the case itself but simply redirected its consideration to the States.

III. Constitutional Intent

Section 1. The Constitution establishes a federal government by and between the multiple States. Powers are enumerated and extended to the federal government by the States. Words used to describe execution of powers are limited to the object of those words which are those powers enumerated in Article I, Section 8

Section 2. The Bill of Rights defines constitutional protections for individuals and certain institutions from government persecution and does not apply or extend to other legal entities.

Section 3. Amendment XIV does not apply to persons born in the United States to parents who are in the country illegally but to persons born to those citizens or legal residents as defined by Congress.

The integrity of the Constitution may be maintained only through application of intellectual legal scholarship to the intent of the founders and to the words used in its construction and their natural meaning. There is flexibility for the interpretation of the Constitution within these defined limits, to address an evolving society and advancement in technology. Nonetheless, the definition of judicial limits discourages the court from infringing on the powers and responsibilities of the other branches of government as well as the States and the people's right to expand the Constitution through amendment. In particular, words used to describe the implementation of federal powers must be limited to the application of those enumerated powers. If they are not, those words will be used to make federal powers unlimited, thereby invalidating the Constitution and undermining the nation.

Children born to parents who reside in the United States illegally are themselves illegally in the country. Illegal behavior cannot encourage or reward violation of our laws with automatic citizenship.

IV. National Crisis and Military Authority

The President may exercise, upon his own authority, extraordinary powers including committing troops to foreign soil or allocation of other federal resources for no more than ninety days without a declaration of a state of emergency or war by Congress. Such declarations may only extend for a period of one year without further congressional approval. No armed forces of the United States shall be placed under command of any foreigner, foreign country or organization.

Congress alone has the constitutional power to declare war. Constitutional powers cannot be delegated. Following World War II and the Cold War policy of mutually assured destruction, armed conflicts were no longer characterized by all-out war but by regional conflicts managed with military force. Regardless, Congress must recognize the intent of the Constitution and retain the authority and responsibility that comes with commitment of U.S. troops to armed conflict. During a period of uncontrolled budget deficits, Congress must assume direct responsibility for funds committed to disasters, whether domestic or foreign, natural or manmade, military or humanitarian. To ensure continued support for national policy and the associated costs over extended periods of time, Congress must be required to annually reaffirm commitment to those policies.

U.S. forces have been placed under foreign command only one time in the history of the country. This resulted in the tragic death of eighteen American soldiers and the desecration of many of their bodies in the streets of Mogadishu, Somalia, followed by the immediate and unconditional retreat of US forces.

V. Fiduciary Responsibility

Section 1. The federal budget will be balanced on or before the fifth fiscal year following ratification of this amendment after which Congress shall establish annual budgets not to exceed total revenues collected during the previous fiscal year. The national debt at the end of the first fiscal year for which there is a balanced budget will be retired in full over twenty years with the burden of repayment distributed equally among each fiscal year.

Section 2. No elected official may be exempt or receive special consideration from any bill for the purpose of raising revenue.

Politicians and the federal government have demonstrated that they are not able to manage the national budget or apply recognized and proven methods of accounting or accountability. The national debt will bankrupt the United States, to the peril of the nation and future generations. We must take responsibility, accept the consequences for our failures, and exercise the strength necessary from our citizens and our politicians to correct our fiscal course. National solvency must be placed ahead of all other domestic considerations, the only exception being military security.

The people must be protected from the avarice of politicians.

VI. Federal Budget

Section 1. All bills for raising revenue shall indicate the specific use of the revenue and shall expire upon the satisfaction of that purpose or within five years barring further legislation.

Section 2. No bill for expenditures introduced in the House of Representatives may be brought to a final vote within less than seven days of publication following attachment of any provision to specify the use of the funds or for additional funding.

Section 3. Monies borrowed against the credit of the United

States shall not exceed 20 percent of GDP except during declarations of war or national crisis as determined by the Senate. Following the assumption of national debt for these acute purposes, the amount of debt exceeding 20 percent of GDP must be repaid in full within one year or a period of months not to exceed twice the duration of the crisis or war whichever is greater.

The people must be protected from the government imposing taxes or fees for a specific purpose and then collecting those revenues in perpetuity regardless of the fulfillment of that purpose. The purpose for bills of revenue must be defined and finite.

Rules must be put in place to discourage the practice of adding attachments to legislation that more often than not represent political pork, projects hidden from the public, and wasteful spending.

National credit must be used wisely and managed effectively. Limitations on national debt must be imposed so that this vital resource is reserved for the protection and perpetuation of the nation.

VII. Restriction on Mandates

Congress shall pass no law requiring implementation or administration by the several States without funding and all necessary resources to satisfy requirements of the law.

State governments are not subordinate to the federal government but parallel with specific responsibilities to local and individual issues. Federal legislation that may be best administered by the State is most likely a responsibility of the State. Nonetheless, that federal legislation that is acceptable to the State or deemed constitutional must include all resources necessary for the State to implement the law.

VIII. Term Limits

Section 1. No person shall be elected to the Senate more than twice, and no person who has held office of Senator, or acted as Senator, for more than three years of a term to which some other person was elected Senator shall be elected to the Senate more than once.

Section 2. No person shall be elected to the House of Representatives more than three times, and no person who has held office as a Representative, or acted as a Representative, for

more than one year of a term to which some other person was
elected shall be elected to the House of Representatives more than
twice.

Term limits must be imposed on the federal
government, because Congress members will not impose
limits on themselves, either by law or voluntarily. Term
limits will eradicate professional politicians and their
harmful practices, improve the practice of democratic
representation, and promote a more active, energetic, and
productive Congress.

IX. Truth in Legislation

*All legislation passed by Congress must include an opinion
indentifying the constitutional authority to pass such legislation.*

A Congress with enumerated powers is one with
defined and limited issues to which legislation may apply.
The U.S. Constitution, amend. 10 states that all powers not
specifically enumerated to Congress are reserved to the
States and the people. Congress has increasingly passed
legislation that encroaches on the powers and
responsibilities of the States, a behavior consistent with the

fears of the founding fathers that all political entities are inclined to increase their power. To clearly demarcate between the powers and responsibilities of the federal and state governments and to ensure a federal government of limited powers, Congress must clearly define those constitutional powers that authorize each piece of legislation under consideration. The proposed Enumerated Powers Act should be raised to the level of an amendment.

X. Rights

Section 1. The United States is founded upon the recognition of divine right s. Congress shall make no law restricting acknowledgement of a higher being.

Section 2. The Constitution establishes a federal government and defines enumerated powers to be exercised in the interest of the multiple States. All language describing the purpose or method for executing federal powers is constrained by the enumerated powers to which they apply.

Section 3. The Bill of Rights protects individuals and certain institutions from government persecution and words used in its construction are constrained by their natural meaning and purpose as originally intended.

Section 4. All Rights not specifically defined in the

Constitution are inherent rights to be expected of all people in a free society and are subject to legislation for the purpose of insuring a secure and stable society.

Recognition of God is not a religion and is an integral part of our nation's founding, history, and future. The United States is not a secular state, but neither is it an ecclesiastical state. Although founded on Judeo-Christian principles, the Constitution specifically bars government from establishing a state religion. This does not exclude representations of God or Judeo-Christian principles in public places or institutions, but it does bar government from requiring acknowledgement or recognition of either.

A constitutional government is one of limited powers. Those limits must be written, recognized, and enforced. To survive as a constitutional republic, the federal government must be limited.

The words of the Constitution have meaning, and the interpretation of those words must be limited to the meaning intended. Without this restriction, words may be given any meaning, which creates confusion, blurs application, and undermines congressional power to legislate. When words are allowed to be redefined, the

Constitution is rendered moot, and the foundation of the nation is uncertain.

Constitutional rights are limited and exist to protect people from government persecution. Expansion of the definition of constitutional rights through definition and interpretation undermines Congress' ability to legislate effectively and muddies understanding and application of rights and laws. It must be assumed in a free society that individuals retain all rights—some of which are subject to legislation, as a condition of citizenship in a stable and secure society, and some of which are protected to prevent persecution by that government. The distinction between constitutional rights and inherent rights subject to legislation must be clear and maintained to ensure integrity in our Constitution, government, and society.

U.S. DECLARATION OF INDEPENDENCE

IN CONGRESS, JULY 4, 1776 *THE UNANIMOUS*
Declaration of the thirteen united States of America.

When in the Course of human events it becomes necessary for one People to dissolve the political bands which have connected them with another and to assume among the powers of the earth, the separate and equal station to which the Laws of Nature and of Nature's God entitle them, a decent respect to the opinions of mankind requires that they should declare the causes which impel them to the separation.

We hold these truths to be self-evident, that all men are created equal, that they are endowed by their Creator with certain unalienable Rights that among these are Life, Liberty and the pursuit of Happiness. — That to secure these rights, Governments are instituted among Men, deriving their just powers from the consent of the governed, — That whenever any Form of Government becomes destructive of these ends, it is the Right of the people to alter or to abolish it, and to institute new Government, laying its foundation on such principles and organizing its powers in such form, as to them shall seem most likely to effect their Safety and Happiness. Prudence, indeed, will dictate that Governments long established should not be changed for light and transient causes; and accordingly all experience hath shewn that mankind are more disposed to suffer, while evils are sufferable than to right themselves by abolishing the forms to which they are accustomed. But when a long train of abuses and usurpations, pursuing invariably the same Object evinces a design to reduce them under absolute Despotism, it is their right, it is their duty, to throw off such Government, and to provide new Guards for their future security. — Such has been the patient sufferance of these Colonies; and such is now the necessity which constrains them to alter their former Systems of Government. The history of the present King of Great Britain is a history of repeated injuries and usurpations, all having in direct object the establishment of an absolute Tyranny over these States. To prove this, let Facts be submitted to a candid world.

He has refused his Assent to Laws, the most wholesome and necessary for the public good.

He has forbidden his Governors to pass Laws of immediate and pressing importance, unless suspended in their operation till his Assent should be obtained; and when so suspended, he has utterly neglected to attend to them.

He has refused to pass other Laws for the accommodation of large districts of people, unless those people would relinquish the right of Representation in the Legislature, a right inestimable to them and formidable to tyrants only.

He has called together legislative bodies at places unusual, uncomfortable, and distant from the depository of their Public Records, for the sole purpose of fatiguing them into compliance with his measures.

He has dissolved Representative Houses repeatedly, for opposing with manly firmness his invasions on the rights of the people.

He has refused for a long time, after such dissolutions, to cause others to be elected, whereby the Legislative Powers, incapable of Annihilation, have returned to the people at large for their exercise; the State remaining in the mean time exposed to all the dangers of invasion from without, and convulsions within.

He has endeavoured to prevent the population of these States; for that purpose obstructing the Laws for Naturalization of Foreigners; refusing to pass others to encourage their migrations hither, and raising the conditions of new Appropriations of Lands.

He has obstructed the Administration of Justice by refusing his Assent to Laws for establishing Judiciary Powers.

He has made Judges dependent on his Will alone for the tenure of their offices, and the amount and payment of their salaries.

He has erected a multitude of New Offices, and sent hither swarms of Officers to harass our people and eat out their substance.

He has kept among us, in times of peace, Standing Armies without the Consent of our legislatures.

He has affected to render the Military independent of and superior to the Civil Power.

He has combined with others to subject us to a jurisdiction foreign to our constitution, and unacknowledged by our laws; giving his Assent to their Acts of pretended Legislation:

For quartering large bodies of armed troops among us:

For protecting them, by a mock Trial from punishment for any Murders which they should commit on the Inhabitants of these States:

For cutting off our Trade with all parts of the world:

For imposing Taxes on us without our Consent:

For depriving us in many cases, of the benefit of Trial by Jury:

For transporting us beyond Seas to be tried for pretended offences:

For abolishing the free System of English Laws in a neighbouring Province, establishing therein an Arbitrary government, and enlarging its Boundaries so as to render it at once an example and fit instrument for introducing the same absolute rule into these Colonies

For taking away our Charters, abolishing our most valuable Laws and altering fundamentally the Forms of our Governments:

For suspending our own Legislatures and declaring themselves invested with power to legislate for us in all cases whatsoever.

He has abdicated Government here, by declaring us out of his Protection and waging War against us.

He has plundered our seas, ravaged our coasts, burnt our towns, and destroyed the lives of our people.

He is at this time transporting large Armies of foreign Mercenaries to compleat the works of death, desolation, and tyranny, already begun with circumstances of Cruelty & Perfidy scarcely paralleled in the most barbarous ages, and totally unworthy the Head of a civilized nation.

He has constrained our fellow Citizens taken Captive on the high Seas to bear Arms against their Country, to become the executioners of their friends and Brethren, or to fall themselves by their Hands.

He has excited domestic insurrections amongst us, and has endeavoured to bring on the inhabitants of our frontiers, the merciless Indian Savages whose known rule of warfare is an undistinguished destruction of all ages, sexes and conditions.

In every stage of these Oppressions We have Petitioned for Redress in the most humble terms: Our repeated Petitions have been answered only by repeated injury. A Prince, whose character is thus marked by every act which may define a Tyrant, is unfit to be the ruler of a free people.

Nor have We been wanting in attentions to our British brethren. We have warned them from time to time of attempts by their legislature to extend an unwarrantable jurisdiction over us. We have reminded them of the circumstances of our emigration and settlement here. We have appealed to their native justice and magnanimity, and we have conjured them by the ties of our common kindred. to disavow these usurpations, which would inevitably interrupt our connections and correspondence. They too have been deaf to the voice of justice and of consanguinity. We must, therefore, acquiesce in the necessity, which denounces our Separation, and hold them, as we hold the rest of mankind, Enemies in War, in Peace Friends.

We, therefore, the Representatives of the united States of America, in General Congress, Assembled, appealing to the Supreme Judge of the world for the rectitude of our intentions, do, in the Name, and by Authority of the good People of these Colonies, solemnly publish and declare, That these united Colonies are, and of Right ought to be Free and Independent States, that they are Absolved from all Allegiance to the British Crown, and that all political connection between them and the State of Great Britain, is and ought to be totally dissolved; and that as Free and Independent States, they have full Power to levy War, conclude Peace contract Alliances, establish Commerce, and to do all other Acts and Things which Independent States may of right do. — And for the support of this Declaration, with a firm reliance on the protection of Divine Providence, we mutually pledge to each other our Lives, our Fortunes and our sacred Honor.

THE CONSTITUTION OF THE UNITED STATES

PREAMBLE

We the people of the United States, in order to form a more perfect union, establish justice, insure domestic tranquility, provide for the common defense, promote the general welfare, and secure the blessings of liberty to ourselves and our posterity, do ordain and establish this Constitution for the United States of America.

Article. I.

Section. 1. All legislative Powers herein granted shall be vested in a Congress of the United States, which shall consist of a Senate and House of Representatives.

Section 2. The House of Representatives shall be composed of Members chosen every second Year by the people of the several States, and the Electors in each State shall have the Qualifications requisite for Electors of the most numerous Branch of the State Legislature.

No Person shall be a Representative who shall not have attained to the Age of twenty five Years, and been seven Years a Citizen of the United States, and who shall not, when elected, be an Inhabitant of that State in which he shall be chosen.

Representatives and direct Taxes shall be apportioned among the several States which may be included within this Union, according to their respective Numbers, which shall be determined by adding to the whole Number of free Persons, including those bound to Service for a Term of Years, and excluding Indians not taxed, three fifths of all other Persons. The actual Enumeration shall be made within three Years after the first Meeting of the Congress of the United States, and within every subsequent Term of ten Years, in such Manner as they shall by Law direct. The number of Representatives shall not exceed one for every thirty Thousand, but each State shall have at Least one Representative; and until such enumeration shall be made, the State of New Hampshire shall be entitled to chuse three, Massachusetts eight, Rhode-Island and Providence Plantations one, Connecticut five, New-York six, New Jersey four, Pennsylvania eight, Delaware one, Maryland six, Virginia ten, North Carolina five, South Carolina five, and Georgia three.

When vacancies happen in the Representation from any State, the Executive Authority thereof shall issue Writs of Election to fill such Vacancies.

The House of Representatives shall chuse their Speaker and other Officers; and shall have the sole Power of Impeachment.

Section 3. The Senate of the United States shall be composed of two Senators from each State, chosen by the Legislature thereof, for six Years; and each Senator shall have one Vote.

Immediately after they shall be assembled in Consequence of the first Election, they shall be divided as equally as may be into three Classes. The Seats of the Senators of the first Class shall be vacated at the Expiration of thc second Year, of the second Class at the Expiration of the fourth Year, and of the third Class at the Expiration of the sixth Year, so that one third may be chosen every second Year; and if Vacancies happen by Resignation, or otherwise, during the Recess of the Legislature of any State, the Executive thereof may make temporary Appointments until the next Meeting of the Legislature, which shall then fill such Vacancies.

No Person shall be a Senator who shall not have attained to the Age of thirty Years, and been nine Years a Citizen of the United States, and who shall not, when elected, be an Inhabitant of that State for which he shall be chosen.

The Vice President of the United States shall be President of the Senate, but shall have no Vote, unless they be equally divided.

The Senate shall chuse their other Officers, and also a President pro tempore, in the Absence of the Vice President, or when he shall exercise the Office of President of the United States.

The Senate shall have the sole Power to try all Impeachments. When sitting for that Purpose, they shall be on

Oath or Affirmation. When the President of the United States is tried, the Chief Justice shall preside: And no Person shall be convicted without the Concurrence of two thirds of the Members present.

Judgment in Cases of Impeachment shall not extend further than to removal from Office, and disqualification to hold and enjoy any Office of honor, Trust or Profit under the United States: but the Party convicted shall nevertheless be liable and subject to Indictment, Trial, Judgment and Punishment, according to Law.

Section 4. The Times, Places and Manner of holding Elections for Senators and Representatives, shall be prescribed in each State by the Legislature thereof; but the Congress may at any time by Law make or alter such Regulations, except as to the Places of chusing Senators.

The Congress shall assemble at least once in every Year, and such Meeting shall be [on the first Monday in December, unless they shall by Law appoint a different Day.

Section 5. Each House shall be the Judge of the Elections, Returns and Qualifications of its own Members, and a Majority of each shall constitute a Quorum to do Business, but a smaller Number may adjourn from day to day, and may be authorized to compel the Attendance of absent Members, in such Manner, and under such Penalties as each House may provide.

Each House may determine the Rules of its Proceedings, punish its Members for disorderly Behaviour, and, with the Concurrence of two thirds, expel a Member.

Each House shall keep a Journal of its Proceedings, and from time to time publish the same, excepting such Parts as may in their Judgment require Secrecy; and the Yeas and Nays of the Members of either House on any question shall, at the Desire of one fifth of those Present, be entered on the Journal.

Neither House, during the Session of Congress, shall, without the Consent of the other, adjourn for more than three days, nor to any other Place than that in which the two Houses shall be sitting.

Section 6. The Senators and Representatives shall receive a Compensation for their Services, to be ascertained by law, and paid out of the Treasury of the United States. They shall in all Cases, except Treason, Felony and Breach of the Peace, be privileged from Arrest during their Attendance at the Session of their respective Houses, and in going to and returning from the same; and for any Speech or Debate in either House, they shall not be questioned in any other Place.

No Senator or Representative shall, during the Time for which he was elected, be appointed to any civil Office under the Authority of the United States, which shall have been created, or the Emoluments whereof shall have been encreased during such time; and no Person holding any Office under the United States, shall be a Member of either House during his Continuance in Office.

Section 7. All Bills for raising Revenue shall originate in the House of Representatives; but the Senate may propose or concur with Amendments as on other Bills.

Every Bill which shall have passed the House of Representatives and the Senate, shall, before it becomes a Law, be presented to the President of the United States; If he approve he shall sign it, but if not he shall return it, with his Objections to that House in which it shall have originated, who shall enter the Objections at large on their Journal, and proceed to reconsider it. If after such Reconsideration two thirds of that House shall agree to pass the Bill, it shall be sent, together with the Objections, to the other House, by which it shall likewise be reconsidered, and if approved by two thirds of that House, it shall become a Law. But in all such Cases the Votes of both Houses shall be determined by Yeas and Nays, and the Names of the Persons voting for and against the Bill shall be entered on the Journal of each House respectively. If any Bill shall not be returned by the President within ten Days (Sundays excepted) after it shall have been presented to him, the Same shall be a Law, in like Manner as if he had signed it, unless the Congress by their Adjournment prevent its Return, in which Case it shall not be a Law.

Every Order, Resolution, or Vote to which the Concurrence of the Senate and House of Representatives may be necessary (except on a question of Adjournment) shall be presented to the President of the United States, and before the Same shall take Effect, shall be approved by him, or being disapproved by him, shall be repassed by two thirds of the Senate and House of Representatives, according to the Rules and Limitations prescribed in the Case of the Bill.

Section 8. The Congress shall have Power To lay and collect Taxes, Duties, Imposts and Excises, to pay the Debts and provide for the common Defence and general Welfare of the United States; but all Duties, Imposts and Excises shall be uniform throughout the United States

To borrow Money on the credit of the United States;

To regulate Commerce with foreign Nations, and among the several States, and with the Indian Tribes;

To establish an uniform [def: constant, unvarying, undeviating] Rule of Naturalization, and uniform Laws on the subject of Bankruptcies throughout the United States;

To coin Money, regulate the Value thereof, and of foreign Coin, and fix the Standard of Weights and Measures;

To provide for the Punishment of counterfeiting the Securities and current Coin of the United States;

To establish Post Offices and post Roads;

To promote the Progress of Science and useful Arts, by securing for limited Times to Authors and Inventors the exclusive Right to their respective Writings and Discoveries;

To constitute Tribunals inferior to the supreme Court;

To define and punish Piracies and Felonies committed on the high Seas, and Offenses against the Law of Nations;

To declare War, grant Letters of Marque and Reprisal, and make Rules concerning Captures on land and Water;

To raise and support Armies, but no Appropriation of Money to that Use shall be for a longer Term than two Years;

To provide and maintain a Navy;

To make Rules for the Government and Regulation of the land and naval Forces;

To provide for calling forth the Militia to execute the Laws of the Union, suppress Insurrections and repel Invasions;

To provide for organizing, arming, and disciplining, the Militia, and for governing such Part of them as may be employed in the Service of the United States, reserving to the States respectively, the Appointment of the Officers, and the Authority of training the Militia according to the discipline prescribed by Congress;

To exercise exclusive Legislation in all Cases whatsoever, over such District (not exceeding ten Miles square) as may, by Cession of particular States, and the Acceptance of Congress, become the Seat of the Government of the United States, and to exercise like Authority over all Places purchased by the Consent of the Legislature of the State in which the Same shall be, for the Erection of Forts, Magazines, Arsenals, dock-Yards and other needful Buildings;--And

To make all Laws which shall be necessary and proper for carrying into Execution the foregoing Powers, and all other Powers vested by this Constitution in the Government of the United States, or in any Department or Officer thereof.

Section 9. The Migration or Importation of such Persons as any of the States now existing shall think proper to admit, shall not be prohibited by the Congress prior to the Year one thousand eight hundred and eight, but a Tax or duty may be imposed on such Importation, not exceeding ten dollars for each Person.

The Privilege of the Writ of Habeas Corpus shall not be suspended, unless when in Cases of Rebellion or Invasion the public Safety may require it.

No Bill of Attainder or ex post facto Law shall be passed.

No Capitation, or other direct, Tax shall be laid, unless in Proportion to the Census or Enumeration herein before directed to be taken.

No Tax or Duty shall be laid on Articles exported from any State.

No Preference shall be given by any Regulation of Commerce or Revenue to the Ports of one State over those of another: nor shall Vessels bound to, or from, one State, be obliged to enter, clear, or pay Duties in another.

No Money shall be drawn from the Treasury, but in Consequence of Appropriations made by Law; and a regular Statement and Account of the Receipts and Expenditures of all public Money shall be published from time to time.

No Title of Nobility shall be granted by the United States: And no Person holding any Office of Profit or Trust under them, shall, without the Consent of the Congress, accept of any present, Emolument, Office, or Title, of any kind whatever, from any King, Prince, or foreign State.

Section 10. No State shall enter into any Treaty, Alliance, or Confederation; grant Letters of Marque and Reprisal; coin Money; emit Bills of Credit; make any Thing but gold and silver Coin a Tender in Payment of Debts; pass any Bill of Attainder, ex post facto Law, or Law impairing the Obligation of Contracts, or grant any Title of Nobility;

No State shall, without the Consent of the Congress, lay any Imposts or Duties on Imports or Exports, except what may be absolutely necessary for executing it's inspection Laws: and the net Produce of all Duties and Imposts, laid by any State on Imports or Exports, shall be for the Use of the Treasury of the United States; and all such Laws shall be subject to the Revision and Controul of the Congress.

No State shall, without the Consent of Congress, lay any Duty of Tonnage, keep Troops, or Ships of War in time of Peace, enter into any Agreement or Compact with another State, or with a foreign Power, or engage in War, unless actually invaded, or in such imminent Danger as will not admit of delay.

Article II

Section 1. The executive power shall be vested in a President of the United States of America. He shall hold his office during the term of four years, and, together with the Vice President, chosen for the same term, be elected, as follows:

Each state shall appoint, in such manner as the Legislature thereof may direct, a number of electors, equal to the whole number of Senators and Representatives to which the State may be entitled in the Congress: but no Senator or Representative, or person holding an office of trust or profit under the United States, shall be appointed an elector.

The electors shall meet in their respective states, and vote by ballot for two persons, of whom one at least shall not be an inhabitant of the same state with themselves. And they shall make a list of all the persons voted for, and of the number of votes for each; which list they shall sign and certify, and transmit sealed to the seat of the government of the United States, directed to the President of the Senate. The President of the Senate shall, in the presence of the Senate and House of Representatives, open all the certificates, and the votes shall then be counted. The person having the greatest number of votes shall be the President, if such number be a majority of the whole number of electors appointed; and if there be more than one who have such majority, and have an equal number of votes, then the House of Representatives shall immediately choose by ballot one of them for President; and if no person have a majority, then from the five highest on the list the said House shall in like manner choose the President. But in choosing the President, the votes shall be taken by States, the representation from each state having one vote; A quorum for this purpose shall consist of a member or members from two thirds of the states, and a majority of all the states shall be necessary to a choice. In every case, after the choice of the President, the person having the greatest number of votes of the electors shall be the Vice President. But if there should remain two or more who have equal votes, the Senate shall choose from them by ballot the Vice

President.

The Congress may determine the time of choosing the electors, and the day on which they shall give their votes; which day shall be the same throughout the United States.

No person except a natural born citizen, or a citizen of the United States, at the time of the adoption of this Constitution, shall be eligible to the office of President; neither shall any person be eligible to that office who shall not have attained to the age of thirty five years, and been fourteen Years a resident within the United States.

In case of the removal of the President from office, or of his death, resignation, or inability to discharge the powers and duties of the said office, the same shall devolve on the Vice President, and the Congress may by law provide for the case of removal, death, resignation or inability, both of the President and Vice President, declaring what officer shall then act as President, and such officer shall act accordingly, until the disability be removed, or a President shall be elected.

The President shall, at stated times, receive for his services, a compensation, which shall neither be increased nor diminished during the period for which he shall have been elected, and he shall not receive within that period any other emolument from the United States, or any of them.

Before he enter on the execution of his office, he shall take the following oath or affirmation:--"I do solemnly swear (or affirm) that I will faithfully execute the office of President of the United States, and will to the best of my ability, preserve, protect and defend the Constitution of the United States."

Section 2. The President shall be commander in chief of the Army and Navy of the United States, and of the militia of the several states, when called into the actual service of the United States; he may require the opinion, in writing, of the principal officer in each of the executive departments, upon any subject relating to the duties of their respective offices, and he shall have power to grant reprieves and pardons for offenses against the United States, except in cases of impeachment.

He shall have power, by and with the advice and consent of the Senate, to make treaties, provided two thirds of the Senators present concur; and he shall nominate, and by and with the advice and consent of the Senate, shall appoint ambassadors, other public ministers and consuls, judges of the Supreme Court, and all other officers of the United States, whose appointments are not herein otherwise provided for, and which shall be established by law: but the Congress may by law vest the appointment of such inferior officers, as they think proper, in the President alone, in the courts of law, or in the heads of departments.

The President shall have power to fill up all vacancies that may happen during the recess of the Senate, by granting commissions which shall expire at the end of their next session.

Section 3. He shall from time to time give to the Congress information of the state of the union, and recommend to their consideration such measures as he shall judge necessary and expedient; he may, on extraordinary occasions, convene both Houses, or either of them, and in case of disagreement between them, with respect to the time of adjournment, he may adjourn them to such time as he shall think proper; he shall receive ambassadors and other public ministers; he shall take care that the laws be faithfully executed, and shall commission all the officers of the United States.

Section 4. The President, Vice President and all civil officers of the United States, shall be removed from office on impeachment for, and conviction of, treason, bribery, or other high crimes and misdemeanors.

Article III

Section 1. The judicial power of the United States, shall be vested in one Supreme Court, and in such inferior courts as the Congress may from time to time ordain and establish. The judges, both of the supreme and inferior courts, shall hold their offices during good behaviour, and shall, at stated times, receive for their services, a compensation, which shall not be diminished during their continuance in office.

Section 2. The judicial power shall extend to all cases, in law and equity, arising under this Constitution, the laws of the United States, and treaties made, or which shall be made, under their authority;--to all cases affecting ambassadors, other public ministers and consuls;--to all cases of admiralty and maritime jurisdiction;--to controversies to which the United States shall be a party;--to controversies between two or more states;--between a state and citizens of another state;--between citizens of different states;--between citizens of the same state claiming lands under grants of different states, and between a state, or the citizens thereof, and foreign states, citizens or subjects.

In all cases affecting ambassadors, other public ministers and consuls, and those in which a state shall be party, the Supreme Court shall have original jurisdiction. In all the other cases before mentioned, the Supreme Court shall have appellate jurisdiction, both as to law and fact, with such exceptions, and under such regulations as the Congress shall make.

The trial of all crimes, except in cases of impeachment, shall be by jury; and such trial shall be held in the state where the said crimes shall have been committed; but when not committed within any state, the trial shall be at such place or places as the Congress may by law have directed.

Section 3. Treason against the United States, shall consist only in levying war against them, or in adhering to their enemies, giving them aid and comfort. No person shall be convicted of treason unless on the testimony of two witnesses to the same overt act, or on confession in open court.

The Congress shall have power to declare the punishment of treason, but no attainder of treason shall work corruption of blood, or forfeiture except during the life of the person attainted.

Article IV

Section 1. Full faith and credit shall be given in each state to the public acts, records, and judicial proceedings of every other state. And the Congress may by general laws prescribe the manner in which such acts, records, and proceedings shall be proved, and the effect thereof.

Section 2. The citizens of each state shall be entitled to all privileges and immunities of citizens in the several states.

A person charged in any state with treason, felony, or other crime, who shall flee from justice, and be found in another state, shall on demand of the executive authority of the state from which he fled, be delivered up, to be removed to the state having jurisdiction of the crime.

No person held to service or labor in one state, under the laws thereof, escaping into another, shall, in consequence of any law or regulation therein, be discharged from such service or labor, but shall be delivered up on claim of the party to whom such service or labor may be due.

Section 3. New states may be admitted by the Congress into this union; but no new states shall be formed or erected within the jurisdiction of any other state; nor any state be formed by the junction of two or more states, or parts of states, without the consent of the legislatures of the states concerned as well as of the Congress.

The Congress shall have power to dispose of and make all needful rules and regulations respecting the territory or other property belonging to the United States; and nothing in this Constitution shall be so construed as to prejudice any claims of the United States, or of any particular state.

Section 4. The United States shall guarantee to every state in this union a republican form of government, and shall protect each of them against invasion [def: intrusion or encroachment]; and on application of the legislature, or of the executive (when the legislature cannot be convened) against domestic violence.

Article V

The Congress, whenever two thirds of both houses shall deem it necessary, shall propose amendments to this Constitution, or, on the application of the legislatures of two thirds of the several states, shall call a convention for proposing amendments, which, in either case, shall be valid to all intents and purposes, as part of this Constitution, when ratified by the legislatures of three fourths of the several states, or by conventions in three fourths thereof, as the one or the other mode of ratification may be proposed by the Congress; provided that no amendment which may be made prior to the year one thousand eight hundred and eight shall in any manner affect the first and fourth clauses in the ninth section of the first article; and that no state, without its consent, shall be deprived of its equal suffrage in the Senate.

Article VI

All debts contracted and engagements entered into, before the adoption of this Constitution, shall be as valid against the United States under this Constitution, as under the Confederation.

This Constitution, and the laws of the United States which shall be made in pursuance thereof; and all treaties made, or which shall be made, under the authority of the United States, shall be the supreme law of the land; and the judges in every state shall be bound thereby, anything in the Constitution or laws of any State to the contrary notwithstanding.

The Senators and Representatives before mentioned, and the members of the several state legislatures, and all executive and judicial officers, both of the United States and of the several states, shall be bound by oath or affirmation, to support this Constitution; but no religious test shall ever be required as a qualification to any office or public trust under the United States.

Article VII
The ratification of the conventions of nine states, shall be sufficient for the establishment of this Constitution between the states so ratifying the same.

Bill of Rights
Amendment I—Congress shall make no law respecting an establishment of religion, or prohibiting the free exercise thereof; or abridging the freedom of speech, or of the press; or the right of the people peaceably to assemble, and to petition the government for a redress of grievances.

Amendment II—A well regulated militia, being necessary to the security of a free state, the right of the people to keep and bear arms, shall not be infringed.

Amendment III—No soldier shall, in time of peace be quartered in any house, without the consent of the owner, nor in time of war, but in a manner to be prescribed by law.

Amendment IV—The right of the people to be secure in their persons, houses, papers, and effects, against unreasonable searches and seizures, shall not be violated, and no warrants shall issue, but upon probable cause, supported by oath or affirmation, and particularly describing the place to be searched, and the persons or things to be seized.

Amendment V—No person shall be held to answer for a capital, or otherwise infamous crime, unless on a presentment or indictment of a grand jury, except in cases arising in the land or naval forces, or in the militia, when in actual service in time of war or public danger; nor shall any person be subject for the same offense to be twice put in jeopardy of life or limb; nor shall be compelled in any criminal case to be a witness against himself, nor be deprived of life, liberty, or property, without due process of law; nor shall private property be taken for public use, without just compensation.

Amendment VI — In all criminal prosecutions, the accused shall enjoy the right to a speedy and public trial, by an impartial jury of the state and district wherein the crime shall have been committed, which district shall have been previously ascertained by law, and to be informed of the nature and cause of the accusation; to be confronted with the witnesses against him; to have compulsory process for obtaining witnesses in his favor, and to have the assistance of counsel for his defense.

Amendment VII — In suits at common law, where the value in controversy shall exceed twenty dollars, the right of trial by jury shall be preserved, and no fact tried by a jury, shall be otherwise reexamined in any court of the United States, than according to the rules of the common law.

Amendment VIII — Excessive bail shall not be required, nor excessive fines imposed, nor cruel and unusual punishments inflicted.

Amendment IX — The enumeration in the Constitution, of certain rights, shall not be construed to deny or disparage others retained by the people.

Amendment X — The powers not delegated to the United States by the Constitution, nor prohibited by it to the states, are reserved to the states respectively, or to the people.

Amendment XI — The judicial power of the United States shall not be construed to extend to any suit in law or equity, commenced or prosecuted against one of the United States by citizens of another state, or by citizens or subjects of any foreign state.

Amendment XII — The electors shall meet in their respective states and vote by ballot for President and Vice-President, one of whom, at least, shall not be an inhabitant of the same state with themselves; they shall name in their ballots the person voted for as President, and in distinct ballots the person voted for as Vice-President, and they shall make distinct lists of all persons voted for as President, and of all persons voted for as Vice-President, and of the number of votes for each, which lists they shall sign and certify, and transmit sealed to the seat of the government of the United States, directed to the President of the Senate;--The President of the Senate shall, in the presence of the Senate and House of Representatives, open all the certificates and the votes shall then be counted;--the person having the greatest number of votes for President, shall be the President, if such number be a majority of the whole number of electors appointed; and if no person have such majority, then from the persons having the highest numbers not exceeding three on the list of those voted for as President, the House of Representatives shall choose immediately, by ballot, the President. But in choosing the President, the votes shall be taken by states, the representation from each state having one vote; a quorum for this purpose shall consist of a member or members from two-thirds of the states, and a majority of all the states shall be necessary to a choice. And if the House of Representatives shall not choose a President whenever the right of choice shall devolve upon them, before the fourth day of March next following, then the Vice-President shall act as President, as in the case of the death or other constitutional disability of the President. The person having the greatest number of votes as Vice-President, shall be the Vice-President, if such number be a majority of the whole number of electors appointed, and if no person have a majority, then from the two highest numbers on the list, the Senate shall choose the Vice-President; a quorum for the purpose shall consist of two-thirds of the whole number of Senators, and a majority of the whole number shall be necessary to a choice. But no person constitutionally ineligible to the office of President shall be eligible to that of Vice-President of the United States.

Amendment XIII — Section 1. Neither slavery nor

involuntary servitude, except as a punishment for crime whereof the party shall have been duly convicted, shall exist within the United States, or any place subject to their jurisdiction.

Section 2. Congress shall have power to enforce this article by appropriate legislation.

Amendment XIV —Section 1. All persons born or naturalized in the United States, and subject to the jurisdiction thereof, are citizens of the United States and of the state wherein they reside. No state shall make or enforce any law which shall abridge the privileges or immunities of citizens of the United States; nor shall any state deprive any person of life, liberty, or property, without due process of law; nor deny to any person within its jurisdiction the equal protection of the laws.

Section 2. Representatives shall be apportioned among the several states according to their respective numbers, counting the whole number of persons in each state, excluding Indians not taxed. But when the right to vote at any election for the choice of electors for President and Vice President of the United States, Representatives in Congress, the executive and judicial officers of a state, or the members of the legislature thereof, is denied to any of the male inhabitants of such state, being twenty-one years of age, and citizens of the United States, or in any way abridged, except for participation in rebellion, or other crime, the basis of representation therein shall be reduced in the proportion which the number of such male citizens shall bear to the whole number of male citizens twenty-one years of age in such state.

Section 3. No person shall be a Senator or Representative in Congress, or elector of President and Vice President, or hold any office, civil or military, under the United States, or under any state, who, having previously taken an oath, as a member of Congress, or as an officer of the United States, or as a member of any state legislature, or as an executive or judicial officer of any state, to support the Constitution of the United States, shall have engaged in insurrection or rebellion against the same, or given aid or comfort to the enemies thereof. But Congress may by a vote of two-thirds of each House, remove such disability.

Section 4. The validity of the public debt of the United States, authorized by law, including debts incurred for payment of pensions and bounties for services in suppressing insurrection or rebellion, shall not be questioned. But neither the United States nor any state shall assume or pay any debt or obligation incurred in aid of insurrection or rebellion against the United States, or any claim for the loss or emancipation of any slave; but all such debts, obligations and claims shall be held illegal and void.

Section 5. The Congress shall have power to enforce, by appropriate legislation, the provisions of this article.

Amendment XV—Section 1. The right of citizens of the United States to vote shall not be denied or abridged by the United States or by any state on account of race, color, or previous condition of servitude.

Section 2. The Congress shall have power to enforce this article by appropriate legislation.

Amendment XVI—The Congress shall have power to lay and collect taxes on incomes, from whatever source derived, without apportionment among the several states, and without regard to any census or enumeration.

Amendment XVII—The Senate of the United States shall be composed of two Senators from each state, elected by the people thereof, for six years; and each Senator shall have one vote. The electors in each state shall have the qualifications requisite for electors of the most numerous branch of the state legislatures.

When vacancies happen in the representation of any state in the Senate, the executive authority of such state shall issue writs of election to fill such vacancies: Provided, that the legislature of any state may empower the executive thereof to make temporary appointments until the people fill the vacancies by election as the legislature may direct.

This amendment shall not be so construed as to affect the election or term of any Senator chosen before it becomes valid as part of the Constitution.

Amendment XVIII — Section 1. After one year from the ratification of this article the manufacture, sale, or transportation of intoxicating liquors within, the importation thereof into, or the exportation thereof from the United States and all territory subject to the jurisdiction thereof for beverage purposes is hereby prohibited.

Section 2. The Congress and the several states shall have concurrent power to enforce this article by appropriate legislation.

Section 3. This article shall be inoperative unless it shall have been ratified as an amendment to the Constitution by the legislatures of the several states, as provided in the Constitution, within seven years from the date of the submission hereof to the states by the Congress.

Amendment XIX — The right of citizens of the United States to vote shall not be denied or abridged by the United States or by any state on account of sex.

Congress shall have power to enforce this article by appropriate legislation.

Amendment XX — Section 1. The terms of the President and Vice President shall end at noon on the 20th day of January, and the terms of Senators and Representatives at noon on the 3d day of January, of the years in which such terms would have ended if this article had not been ratified; and the terms of their successors shall then begin.

Section 2. The Congress shall assemble at least once in every year, and such meeting shall begin at noon on the 3d day of

January, unless they shall by law appoint a different day.

Section 3. If, at the time fixed for the beginning of the term of the President, the President elect shall have died, the Vice President elect shall become President. If a President shall not have been chosen before the time fixed for the beginning of his term, or if the President elect shall have failed to qualify, then the Vice President elect shall act as President until a President shall have qualified; and the Congress may by law provide for the case wherein neither a President elect nor a Vice President elect shall have qualified, declaring who shall then act as President, or the manner in which one who is to act shall be selected, and such person shall act accordingly until a President or Vice President shall have qualified.

Section 4. The Congress may by law provide for the case of the death of any of the persons from whom the House of Representatives may choose a President whenever the right of choice shall have devolved upon them, and for the case of the death of any of the persons from whom the Senate may choose a Vice President whenever the right of choice shall have devolved upon them.

Section 5. Sections 1 and 2 shall take effect on the 15th day of October following the ratification of this article.

Section 6. This article shall be inoperative unless it shall have been ratified as an amendment to the Constitution by the legislatures of three-fourths of the several states within seven years from the date of its submission.

Amendment XXI — Section 1. The eighteenth article of amendment to the Constitution of the United States is hereby repealed.

Section 2. The transportation or importation into any state, territory, or possession of the United States for delivery or use therein of intoxicating liquors, in violation of the laws thereof, is hereby prohibited.

Section 3. This article shall be inoperative unless it shall have been ratified as an amendment to the Constitution by conventions in the several states, as provided in the Constitution, within seven years from the date of the submission hereof to the states by the Congress.

Amendment XXII — Section 1. No person shall be elected to the office of the President more than twice, and no person who has held the office of President, or acted as President, for more than two years of a term to which some other person was elected President shall be elected to the office of the President more than once. But this article shall not apply to any person holding the office of President when this article was proposed by the Congress, and shall not prevent any person who may be holding the office of President, or acting as President, during the term within which this article becomes operative from holding the office of President or acting as President during the remainder of such term.

Section 2. This article shall be inoperative unless it shall have been ratified as an amendment to the Constitution by the legislatures of three-fourths of the several states within seven years from the date of its submission to the states by the Congress.

Amendment XXIII — Section 1. The District constituting the seat of government of the United States shall appoint in such manner as the Congress may direct:

A number of electors of President and Vice President equal to the whole number of Senators and Representatives in Congress to which the District would be entitled if it were a state, but in no event more than the least populous state; they shall be in addition to those appointed by the states, but they shall be considered, for the purposes of the election of President and Vice President, to be electors appointed by a state; and they shall meet in the District and perform such duties as provided by the twelfth article of amendment.

Section 2. The Congress shall have power to enforce this article by appropriate legislation.

Amendment XXIV — Section 1. The right of citizens of the United States to vote in any primary or other election for President or Vice President, for electors for President or Vice President, or for Senator or Representative in Congress, shall not be denied or abridged by the United States or any state by reason of failure to pay any poll tax or other tax.

Section 2. The Congress shall have power to enforce this article by appropriate legislation.

Amendment XXV — Section 1. In case of the removal of the President from office or of his death or resignation, the Vice President shall become President.

Section 2. Whenever there is a vacancy in the office of the Vice President, the President shall nominate a Vice President who shall take office upon confirmation by a majority vote of both Houses of Congress.

Section 3. Whenever the President transmits to the President pro tempore of the Senate and the Speaker of the House of Representatives his written declaration that he is unable to discharge the powers and duties of his office, and until he transmits to them a written declaration to the contrary, such powers and duties shall be discharged by the Vice President as Acting President.

Section 4. Whenever the Vice President and a majority of either the principal officers of the executive departments or of such other body as Congress may by law provide, transmit to the President pro tempore of the Senate and the Speaker of the House of Representatives their written declaration that the President is unable to discharge the powers and duties of his office, the Vice President shall immediately assume the powers and duties of the office as Acting President.

Thereafter, when the President transmits to the President pro tempore of the Senate and the Speaker of the House of Representatives his written declaration that no inability exists, he shall resume the powers and duties of his office unless the Vice President and a majority of either the principal officers of the executive department or of such other body as Congress may by law provide, transmit within four days to the President pro tempore of the Senate and the Speaker of the House of Representatives their written declaration that the President is unable to discharge the powers and duties of his office. Thereupon Congress shall decide the issue, assembling within forty-eight hours for that purpose if not in session. If the Congress, within twenty-one days after receipt of the latter written declaration, or, if Congress is not in session, within twenty-one days after Congress is required to assemble, determines by two-thirds vote of both Houses that the President is unable to discharge the powers and duties of his office, the Vice President shall continue to discharge the same as Acting President; otherwise, the President shall resume the powers and duties of his office.

Amendment XXVI—Section 1. The right of citizens of the United States, who are 18 years of age or older, to vote, shall not be denied or abridged by the United States or any state on account of age.

Section 2. The Congress shall have the power to enforce this article by appropriate legislation.

Amendment XXVII—No law, varying the compensation for the services of the Senators and Representatives, shall take effect, until an election of Representatives shall have intervened.

RESOURCES

You may purchase this book online in paperback at
https://www.createspace.com/3442955

Ten Amendments Blog:
http://tenamendmentstosaveamerica.blogspot.com

For further information about this subject, for interviews, or to purchase this book at a volume discount, contact W. Davis Jones at djones4193@gmail.com.

www.ingramcontent.com/pod-product-compliance
Lightning Source LLC
Chambersburg PA
CBHW020434290526
45785CB00002B/838